Family Sun Signs

*How Your Sun Sign Blends or Conflicts
With Your Family*

Adam Fronteras

A Sterling/Zambezi Book
Sterling Publishing Co., Inc
New York

Illustrations: Jonathan Dee
Cover design: Jan Budkowski
Editor: Sasha Fenton

Library of Congress Cataloging-in-Publication Data Available
Fronteras, Adam.
    Family sun signs : how you blend or conflict with your loved ones
    / by Adam Fronteras ; illustreated by Jonathan Dee.
      p. cm.
    Includes index.
    ISBN 1-4027-0191-8
    1. Astrology. 2. Family—Miscellanea. I. Title.

BF1729.F35 F76 2002
133.5'2—dc21

                                                        2002066943

        2   4   6   8   10   9   7   5   3   1

        Published by Sterling Publishing Company, Inc.
        387 Park Avenue South, New York, NY 10016
      First published in Great Britain by Zambezi Publishing
                © 2002 by Adam Fronteras
          Distributed in Canada by Sterling Publishing
  c/o Canadian Manda Group, One Atlantic Avenue, Suite 105
            Toronto, Ontario, Canada M6K 3E7
  Distributed in Australia by Capricorn Link (Australia) Pty. Ltd.
        P.O. Box 704, Windsor, NSW 2756 Australia

Sterling ISBN 1-4027-0191-8

Contents

Families and Astrology

Most popular astrology books are predominantly aimed at you yourself, although some also deal with compatibility between you and your partner. This book is a little different, in that it explores your own character plus the nature of all those who are around you. My book looks at the way you relate to others in your family or your extended family circle. You can double the value of this book by studying each sun sign type on its own merits, then you can check out the way that you relate to each of your relatives and also how they relate to each other.

This book will enable you to discover how you prepare for pregnancy and a coming child, and to learn about the nature and personalities of your children - in addition to your partner's quirks. Uniquely, this book explores relationships with parents and in-laws, and it shows you how to ensure that the older generation remains part of your family life. Having said this, the emphasis will be placed upon the level of involvement that you wish to set, rather than trying to force you to accommodate a difficult parent or in-law. I then take a glance at how you will fare with grandchildren and also with sibling relationships.

If yours is a non-nuclear family, you will need to use a bit of common sense to work out whether a person feels more like a blood relative or an in-law; then you can choose which section you wish to read. The child segments may throw useful light on any awkwardness that arises between you and a stepchild or even a half-sister or brother.

Finally, I offer you a bit of fun by looking at the kind of pet you would prefer, and then at that mechanical object that is so often a part of the family, complete with its own pet name - your automobile! Believe it or not, the information on sun signs and vehicles comes from two motor insurance companies, SAGA in Britain and the Royal and Sun Alliance, which is worldwide.

Just as people have relationships with each other, so do the planets and the zodiac signs. Many articles and books on astrology suggest that love relationships work best among people of the same element, but we will look at this in more detail in the relevant chapters. As an overview, if you are an Aries, Leo or Sagittarius, you belong to the element of fire, which endows you with drive, energy and an inclination to stand up for your ideas and beliefs, allied to a taste for action and adventure. Taurus, Virgo and Capricorn belong to the element of earth, so if you belong to these signs, you are practical and sensible, strong-willed, determined, reliable and solid. Gemini, Libra and Aquarius are the air signs that intellectual and fun loving people, keen to try new things, belong to, and if you belong to this group, you probably find it hard to keep still. Lastly, we have the water signs of Cancer, Scorpio and Pisces; if you belong to one of these sensitive and caring signs, you tend to be intuitive, imaginative, idealistic and sometimes rather emotional.

Astrologers say that signs in the same elements work well together - and they do. However, relationships can break down even when couples share interests, hobbies and lifestyles. Sometimes people with completely different signs and elements that register completely different outlooks, interests and inspirations, suit each other better than those who are near clones of each other. Sure enough, there can be as many problems due to being too much alike as there are in being different. This book explores the way that the elemental groups work together within a family and the chances of success or failure, not only for lovers but also within the huge variety of family relationships.

As adults, we have a different relationship with our parents than we did when we were children. So here you can refer both to the relationship you can expect to have with your child and vice versa. Then you can move on to discover the energies that lie behind your own relationships with parents, in-laws or other parental figures in your adulthood. All the relationships in this book are based on the elemental building blocks in astrology. It is so often your sun sign element and that of the people to whom you are closest that dictate each individual's outlook and reactions - and also the way that each relationship works.

How Does Astrology Work?

There is no hard evidence as to how astrology works from a scientific point of view. There is statistical evidence to show that astrology does work, although this concentrates on astrological research and the impact that certain planets, signs and astrological houses have, but this doesn't show how it works.

The first theory is magnetic or gravitational force. It is known that the sun and the moon affect the tides and the reactions of animals. It is also known that sun spot activity and the positions of the major planets like Jupiter can affect radio reception. Our brain is a mass of electronic impulses, so if a radio can be affected our far more sensitive mind could be equally affected. Astronomers dismiss the gravitational effect of the planets, as there is less gravitational pull on the human body than that of a double-decker bus a few streets away. A second theory that many astrologers and the few scientists who believe in astrology (such as Professor Percy Seymour of Plymouth University), is that the planets may issue some form of vibration or electrical energy. Each planet operates on a slightly different frequency and our brain responds to these frequencies, so just as a radio can be tuned into a particular frequency it is possible that we also resonate to planetary and stellar frequencies.

The third theory is that the gods created the heavens above to mirror life on earth in a synchronistic way. The old adage "as above, so below" presents human beings as part of a galactic jigsaw, with the movement in the skies above directly affecting the movement of individuals below.

A fourth theory is that it astrology induces some kind of psychic ability. Casting the chart and looking at the positions of the planets directs our minds towards a higher form of communication. This theory suggests that astrologers use astrological charts as a kind of crutch that allows the mind to switch into pure psychic mode, and that astrology works in the same way as using crystal balls, tea-leaves or Tarot cards does. Certainly, that could apply to some personal readings, but computer astrology readings also show a high degree of accuracy. Not all astrologers are psychic, and even those who are can find it difficult to work out math, calculate, use psychology, talk to a client and be psychic at the same time - especially when giving a reading over the telephone. Having said this, no computer printout can compare to a personal reading with a good astrologer.

Yet another theory is that the gods direct our activities, and the planets merely act as a cosmic clock that marks time, in the same way as do the hands on a clock or the dates on a calendar. A clock or calendar cannot make anything happen, they cannot even make time happen - they simply mark its passing.

I cannot give you an exact reason why astrology works but here is my opinion for what it is worth. All the planets have an electric field and so does everything on earth. The planets and our bodies notice changes in those electrical fields. The argument is that the planets are so far away as to have little influence on us, but their light reaches us, so maybe a little of their electrical energy also reaches us.

The comparison that I always like to make is with the medical practice of homeopathy. This is where a medicinal product is diluted to such an extent that there is only a miniscule amount of the original substance left. There have been tests to show in homeopathy that some of the drugs have been so diluted that they are not actually traceable in the actual liquid or tablets given to the patient - but still it works. Homeopaths will tell you that it is because there is an essence or vibration of the substance present, and the same idea can be applied to the way that I feel about astrology. This essence of the planet's original energy or the essence or vibration of that zodiac sign can have an effect on us - and the planets themselves absorb energies from distant stars of different magnitudes. Countless astrologers down the ages from Babylonian times and beyond have observed and recorded these stellar movements and their effects on people. These observations have arrived at the blueprint for each of us. The movement of the planets that astrologers call transits, the angles that they make to each other, the places where their magnetic influences collide and mix all exert an effect on our daily lives.

Going back to my earlier comparison with homeopathy and the theory that the weaker the dilution of the active drug, the stronger it becomes; and this works very well with my views on astrology. The outer planets such as Pluto and Neptune have more far-reaching effects on our lives than some of the inner planets like Mercury and Venus or even our close neighbor, the moon. In astrological terms, these nearby planets tend to show a passing phase rather than a long-term change or problem area of life. There are some that believe that homeopathy has no place in medicine, but in recent years the interest and scientific acceptance has grown. Just as homeopathy is now a form of alternative medicine that is actually available on the National Health Service in the UK, and it is an accepted form of treatment for many private healthcare insurance companies, so perhaps one day, astrology will also become accepted by the mainstream.

But this cannot be the whole answer, otherwise a computer would be able to give perfect readings. Certainly the interpretation programs have improved tremendously over the last fifteen years and no doubt they will continue to improve, but astrology in its magnetic or electrical resonance is only a blueprint. Real life astrologers tend to get much more out of a chart than any computer can. I believe that this is where an astrologer's knowledge of human psychology, intuition or even psychic ability comes in. Everyone has a psychic faculty to a certain extent. Perhaps was prevalent in pre-history, when humans had to rely on their acute heightened sense of awareness about danger or where to find food and water. Language is a recent development in terms of human evolution, so perhaps early humans communicated far more by instinct and feelings. Despite the fact that we all have intuition and psychic ability, there are some who develop it more than others. As with artistic skills, we can all learn them to a certain extent but only some of us will become great and inspirational. If you decide that you really want in depth astrological consultation for yourself or your family, do not hesitate to contact the author on adam@adamfronteras, co.uk.

You would be surprised if you knew how many big companies and institutions use astrology from helping to plot market trends for financial investment or for the recruitment of the right candidate for a job. Astrologers have long used these methods to compare relationships, not only between partners but also between parents and children, so there is nothing new or revolutionary about the concept behind this book, only in the fact that it encompasses the whole family's stars and elements. This book will teach you the basics of how to understand yourself and your relations. It won't cure all problems but it will offer valuable insight into your family situation.

After working in the field for over a quarter of a century, I still can't give you a precise reason why astrology works - all I know is that it just does!

A Short History of Astrology

The Birth of Astrology

Astrology's birthplace was Mesopotamia, in the fertile area between the Tigris and Euphrates rivers in the land that is now known as Iraq. This was the area where, at the end of the last ice age, a mutation occurred in the natural grasses of the earth, allowing man to cultivate crops that could be stored and used for feeding himself and also for feeding his animals. The need to take animals from one grassy area to another at the change of each season came to an end; so man began to settle into an agricultural way of life in the form that it is still known in many parts of the world. The ability to store food allowed the population of a town to grow and to divide into those who dealt with agriculture and those who kept accounts or performed other duties, and this allowed the foundation of towns and civilization. Man soon began to concentrate on studying such things as mathematics, writing, creating primitive clocks and calendars, to perform religious or shaman duties - and, of course, to study the stars.

During the third millennium B.C. this fertile area was the center of the Chaldean Empire. The Chaldeans studied stars to such an extent that the word Chaldean became synonymous with the word astrologer. Later in the same part of the world, Babylonian priests recorded the motions and the movements of the planets. From this time until the beginnings of science, astronomy and astrology were one and the same subject. Gradually, characteristics were ascribed to the planets. It was noted that the planets followed the trajectory of the sun, which is known as the ecliptic. Later the star patterns that were arrayed around the ecliptic became known as the zodiac. The word zodiac comes from the ancient Greek word for animal. The term horoscope derives from the Greek hora meaning time and skopos meaning observer. The oldest known observers date back to 412 B.C., which was the start of astrology for individuals rather than kings, military leaders, or for working out the right time to plant or harvest crops.

Egypt

Astrology spread from Babylon to Egypt, and it was the Greek historian, Herodotus, who wrote about the Egyptian astrologers. Naturally, astrology traveled to Athens and then to Rome. Julius Caesar took the sign of Taurus as his emblem, while Augustus Caesar had the sign of Capricorn stamped on his silver coins. Each of the imperial chariots in the stadium belonged to twelve different stables. Each bearing a sign of the zodiac, while each of the lanes that the chariots raced along was dedicated to one of the planets - as were the seven days of the week. Around 130 A.D. Ptolemy created the Ptolemaic system that held the theory that the earth was the center of the universe and all the planets circled around it. He also created the Tetrabiblos or Three Books, which was a compilation of works on astrology.

Rome

Astrology entered Rome during the last decades of the Republic and it flourished under the Caesars. During the reign of Augustus, Rome was almost swept free of astrologers and prophets on the Emperor's personal orders. The prohibition continued with increased severity under the reign of Tiberius, when both the astrologer and his client were liable to be executed if they were discovered or denounced. However, by the end of the first century AD, astrology completely dominated in Rome, almost achieving the status of a religion. Once again, astrologers were expelled from Rome by Claudius, but then the importation of religions from the east resulted in yet another renaissance for astrology.

The Arabs

As Christianity grew, astrology fell into disrepute. Though in the Arab world, astrology was considered so important that Arabs built many observatories, and it is noteworthy that the crescent moon and star still figure in many Islamic flags.

The Death of Astrology

Early Christianity was permeated with astrological theory until Christianity began to turn the gods of Olympus into the devils of hell, for instance by transforming Pan into Satan. The theories and practices of astrology were considered to be malevolent pagan influences. By the end of the fourth century, astrology was in retreat and it was proscribed as demonic. St. Augustine led the attack on astrology. In his youth he had consulted astrologers and shared the common belief in their art, but this belief was undermined by the discovery that a wealthy landowner had been born at the same time as a slave on his estate. After this, he claimed that astrology was a fraud and delusion that usurped God's power over the universe. For the next four centuries astrology was dismissed, although it was still kept alive by a small underground movement.

The Middle Ages

Astrology eventually found its way back into Europe, and academics and scientists such as Albertus Magnus (1200-1280 A.D.) and his disciple Thomas Aquinas studied it. By this time, astrology was confined to the nobility, and very few sovereigns chose to rule without an astrologer's advice. Astrology first reappeared in Italy, and it was Guido Bonatto who revived it by publishing a popular book, which was a mixture of Greek and Arab learning. This contained his interpretations of classic astrological systems. By the end of his lifetime, an astrologer was a respected professional, sharing the lecture dais with astronomers and physicians.

The Renaissance

During the renaissance, the study of witchcraft, alchemy and astrology began to rise. All three had been present in the background of European culture, but now they moved to center stage, and astrology was supported by the most brilliant and influential figures of the period. Most universities had a chair in astrology and wealthy families often paid a retainer to the most successful astrologer in their area.

The development of science changed people's view of the planets. Copernicus recognized that the sun was at the center of the planetary positions, and had to suffer house imprisonment and a veritable intefada by the Pope as a result of this discovery! The discoveries of Copernicus, Keppler and Galileo failed to make any difference to popular thought. The position of the planets relative to the earth remained unaltered, and solar influence was unaffected by the fact it came from a fixed rather than a moving source. Many of these astronomers financed their interests by writing books with astrological predictions - indeed, Keppler called astronomy the "good mother" and astrology the "bad daughter", because he saw the latter as a lower form of the former.

Elizabethan England

In England astrology was brought to the fore once again during Elizabeth the First's reign by the work of Doctor John Dee. He had predicted the accession of Elizabeth to the throne, so she invited him to choose an auspicious day for her coronation. He was to occupy an important place at court and he performed a variety of tasks, including sometimes acting as a spy. Shortly after Dee's death, William Lilly was born, and Lilly was destined to be one of the most renowned astrologers ever. He was credited with predicting the great fire of London, and his prediction was so accurate that he was summoned before a Parliamentary Committee and closely questioned!

The Age of Reason

During the eighteenth century the intellectual climate saw astrology sink down to the level of conjurers and fairground charlatans, and in Europe, astrology almost disappeared. In Britain the continuing publication of almanacs allowed it to stay alive, although it had retreated in popularity.

The Nineteenth Century

In early nineteenth century England, astrology was viewed in two opposing manners. One problem was that during and immediately after the Napoleonic Wars, there was a terrible recession and many people starved. Some turned to fortune telling and used this for the purpose of tricking people out of money, which is why parliament then brought in the witchcraft acts that outlawed any form of prediction. Later, a wide variety of crafts and professions discovered that they could appeal to a vastly increased audience through cheaply printed pamphlets. The first astrologer to take advantage of this was Robert Cross Smith, who later became known as Raphael. His prolific writing brought astrology back into the realm of popular culture.

Hot on his heels followed Richard Morrison, writing under the name of Zadkiel. Morrison's work was highly popular, although he went too far and caused a scandal by claiming to be able to speak to the apostles and Christ through the use of a crystal ball. In the late nineteenth century, the USA and Britain saw a rise in the study of occultism. Astrology was deeply affected by this, and astrologers increased in number, falling into two camps - those who saw astrology as a science and those who regarded it as a branch of the occult.

The Theosophical Society came into being in 1875 in New York. Theosophy was more socially acceptable than astrology, and the backing given to astrology by Theosophists raised its profile into that of a respectable occupation. The respectability that astrology had gained encouraged Sigmund Freud and later his pupil, Carl Gustav Jung, to pay attention to astrology.

In the latter years of the nineteenth century, a Theosophist called William Allen, later to be known as Alan Leo, began his mission of carrying astrology into the twentieth century. Leo published a popular astrological magazine and invented cheap horoscopes. Subscribers to his magazine were able to order horoscopes from his office for the price of one shilling. The service was so successful that Leo had to take on a staff of astrologers to compile horoscopes from previously prepared sheets. Leo was twice prosecuted under the witchcraft laws for fortune telling, but he continued to be successful and he wrote numerous astrological books and ran correspondence courses for aspiring astrologers.

The Twentieth Century

During the First World War astrology again declined in Europe, probably due to an understandable terror on the part of ordinary people who didn't want to hear about the future. The next boom in astrology occurred in the USA in the 1930s when Evangeline Adams began broadcasting as the first radio astrologer. Her rise to fame and her popularity had been assured as early as 1914, when she was accused of fortune telling but won the case because she convinced the judge that astrology was a science.

In Britain an accident of fate resurrected astrology. The editor of the Sunday Express newspaper was casting around for a fresh slant on the birth of Princess Margaret, when he lit on the idea of asking astrologer, R. H. Naylor, to provide a horoscope. He followed this up in an article, making the prediction that British aircraft were likely to go through a dangerous period. A few hours after publication the news of the R101 airship disaster broke. Predictive manuals by some of the better-known astrological writers began to appear on the market, and the editor of the Express asked Naylor to find a way of providing a permanent astrology column. Naylor needed to find a way of writing that involved the reader, so he hit on the idea of dividing his writing into twelve paragraphs. This would give each person their particular sun sign to read about. Thus the newspaper astrology column was launched - and shortly afterwards other popular newspapers followed suit.

The biggest blow to strike astrology in this period was the failure of astrologers to predict the Second World War. However, astrology continued to rise in popularity and it was only the shortage of paper that held it back. In Germany, the interest in astrology was intense, but this centered on the study of character through the horoscope as opposed to an emphasis on prediction. Fortune telling was banned under the Nazis from 1934. There is no clear evidence that Hitler was interested in astrology, but it is known that Heinrich Himmler was deeply into all forms of the occult, as was the "official philosopher" of the Nazi party, Adolf Rosenberg. Astrologers worked with the Nazis - although they came to sticky ends when they predicted reversals in fortune after the failure of the Stalingrad campaign in 1942. Just before Hitler killed himself, Goebbels rushed in with a copy of his horoscope and also that of Germany and he told him that an unnamed astrologer had assured him that Germany would survive. He suggested that Hitler should reconsider committing suicide. As I said, Hitler wasn't into astrology - but the astrologer was right, Germany survived and has subsequently prospered.

In Britain, newspaper horoscopes played a part in keeping up morale throughout the Second World War, and after the war the number of astrologers steadily rose. With the arrival of the New Age in the 1960s, astrology again became fashionable. Indeed, by 1969, it was estimated that there were over ten thousand professional astrologers in the United States alone. During the 1960s and 1970s, the first question a stranger would ask was, "What's your sign?"

Although sun sign astrology remains highly popular, astrology in its more traditional and detailed form retains a large amount of interest - and in India in particular, astrology is taken very seriously. Over the last few decades, a large amount of research has been conducted into the validity of astrology, and the work of the statistician Michel Gauquelin is the most widely known. Gauquelin set out to disprove astrology and was astounded to discover that many astrological premises worked.

Nowadays, astrology continues to hold people's attention. Associations, societies and schools abound all over the world. Although most people start by reading sun sign books but many now progress to learning how to use astrological software and to interpret their birthchart and much more. Historians are beginning to explore the documents left by astrologers of the past, and science is beginning to show an interest through the study of natural rhythms.

Just like the kings and queens of the past, a recent American president made use of astrology (although it may have been his wife who was really keen on this idea). Allegedly, practically every major move or important decision was agreed with an astrologer in San Francisco. Shortly before Ronald Reagan was shot in an assassination attempt in 1981, his astrologer prophesied that something bad would happen to him. Nancy Reagan always referred to the astrologer as her "friend".

The following quote is by Donald T. Regan - Ronald Reagan's former Chief of Staff.

"Although I never met this clairvoyant (sic), she had such a significant influence on my work and on the affairs of state that in the end I kept an appointment calendar in different colors on my desk. "Good" days were marked in green, "bad" days in red and "uncertain" days in yellow. I used this aide memoir to be able to plot the opportune moment to send the President of the United States from one place to another, to plan a public appearance for him or to initiate negotiations with a foreign power."

The Elements

When astrologers look at compatibility between people, they often look at the elements because these are the basic building blocks of the zodiac. The elements are fire, earth, air and water, and each of the zodiac signs is assigned to one of these elements. Aries, Leo and Sagittarius are the dynamic fire signs of the zodiac, and people of these signs are full of energy and enthusiasm. Taurus, Virgo and Capricorn are the dependable earth signs of the zodiac, and people of these signs are noted for their stubbornness and precision. The air signs are Gemini, Libra and Aquarius, and people of these signs are the party-goes of the zodiac who are also full of bubbly new ideas. The emotional, caring and intense element of water rules Cancer, Scorpio and Pisces, and these water signs are intense people who can become martyrs for the sake of others.

The Element of Fire
Aries, Leo, Sagittarius

Think of fire bringing light and energy, because people of this element have the same fire and enthusiasm for new ideas. Fire is volatile, and when it is uncontrolled it is dangerous.

Those who were born under this element, are warm, outgoing and a little self-centered. The spark of life makes them very dramatic and these people can see possibilities that others miss, and this makes them successful in life. Once they have grasped an opportunity they run with it, and even if things become tough, they don't give up. Like an ever-developing flame, they can dart towards different ideas and areas of life, so that in a way they manage to twist and turn like the flames in a fire in order to make the most of things. Fire signs enjoy life to the full, they are full of ideas and energy and they tend to do things quickly. Sometimes they have a little too much energy. However, when failure stares them in the face or if life seems too staid, they can actually fall into despair. Fire sign people don't like to plan too rigidly because they need to be able to make changes where necessary. Security is not their main goal because they need to the option of sacrificing some of the permanent aspects of life in favor of adventure.

The Element of Earth
Taurus, Virgo, Capricorn

These are considered to be the practical signs because the element of earth represents foundations.

Earth sign people are realistic and practical; so much so that occasionally their imagination can be stunted - although this is less likely to be the case with Virgo than with Taurus and Capricorn. Earth sign people need to touch something before they can believe in it and they can only believe in something once they themselves have experienced it. These subjects have business acumen and they can do well in financial roles. Earth people have willpower and determination, so they fight hard for what they believe in and they also fight hard in for what they want in work situations or in relationships. These people can be obstinate and dogmatic and it is difficult to get them to change their minds, also they can be a little narrow-minded when it comes to the views of other people.

Earth people don't like change and they may constantly fight it but this has its advantages in that it makes them incredibly loyal. Earth people make loyal and stable lovers, adding stability and conformity to their relationships - which may be a boon to one person and a problem to another. People born under earth signs can often seem very mature for their age and they can act as though they are old even when they are young. They don't like taking risks or being rushed, so they take things at their own pace.

Earth people can believe too much in order and discipline, particularly when looking after children. They want their children to conform to their pattern of life and they may find it difficult to see the advantage in a child finding its own way. However, they are very protective of their offspring.

The Element of Air
Gemini, Libra, Aquarius

These are the freethinking signs of the zodiac and they do not like to be tied down, because they need to be able to explore new ideas and avenues.

Air sign people are generally bright and they use their imagination to achieve their aims. Astrologically speaking, air signs can be difficult to fathom because they are not as obvious or as transparent as those of fire, water and earth - and they tend to hide their feelings. Libra and Aquarius are normally very optimistic and they don't like looking at the bad side of things but Geminis can be real miseries. Even the optimistic air sign types lose their way when they cannot see something working for them by means of logic, because they find it very hard to rely on their instincts. These people can be quite difficult to understand because, just as we can only feel the air when it is blowing hot or cold and we rarely notice anything in between, the same can be said about the characteristics of those born under the air signs. They can go unnoticed for long periods of time and then suddenly become very noticeable.

Air signs like to take their time and to think things over carefully and calmly. Even when working towards something, they tend to start off slowly and gradually speed up. People born under the sign of air can occasionally appear cold and distant, but like the nature of air itself, this can soon change. It often appears that there is more going on in their minds than they are saying. They are not particularly good at talking about their feelings but they make good listeners who are always willing to give good advice. This tendency makes them good lawyers, as they see things objectively and often from a different perspective. Air sign people are free spirits who don't like to feel tied down. They are not the most romantic of characters, so in a relationship they can be over-analytical and intellectual.

The Element of Water
Cancer, Scorpio, Pisces

Water sign people are associated with the deep, feeling side of nature, so those who are born under these signs are ruled by their emotions. They do everything based on what they are feeling, and their intuition and their hearts rule their heads.

Water signs rely on feeling, so they have a strong need to touch and be touched. These subjects are also deeply sensuous and romantic. However, as much as touch is about feeling and sensuality, to them it is also about reassurance. As youngsters, they prefer to study "feeling" subjects such as art, history, literature, music, acting and dancing.

Water signs live for relationships. To be bonded to someone else is their ultimate goal. Although they have the perception to spot when something is going wrong, their need for relationships can sometimes cloud the issue and they don't always have the ability to express their own inner feelings. These subjects can be very moody, as their emotions constantly bounce up and down in their response to situations and people and often this happens for no reason that anyone else can fathom.

Water signs use their intuition, which sometimes makes others consider them to be irrational. They can base their likes or dislikes on the shape of someone's nose, the color of his hair or something else that doesn't appear to be connected to the true nature of the person in question. Water signs have a deep secretive nature. They often hide things from others, but equally, they are clever at digging out the secrets of others. These people are nosy, and if left alone in someone else's house or office, they won't hesitate to rummage through drawers and paperwork.

These subjects make excellent counselors and health therapists, although they can sometimes get too involved, and they need to guard against becoming caught up with other people's problems. Water sign people can deceive others and they can also deceive themselves, so they can hide their emotions from others - and perhaps also shy away from their emotions. For instance, if something is wrong in a relationship, they will ignore it as far as possible, but this gnaws away at their inner feelings until eventually they have to do something about it. On the other hand, when their partner is crying out for a little bit of space and freedom in a relationship, water signs react by clinging ever more tightly and possibly suffocating the relationship. Relationships mean everything to these people, and sometimes their possessiveness, fear of abandonment or need to be the center of the partner's world can mean that they become resentful of everyone else - and this can include children as well as parents and in-laws. As parents, water signs need to be needed and they feel quite bereft when children want to grow up and leave the nest. Difficulties may begin to show themselves when growing children show signs of independence.

The Planetary Rulerships

Each sign is ruled by a planet whose energies are directed into the sign that it rules.

Sign	Traditional	Modern
Aries	Mars	Mars
Taurus	Venus	Venus
Gemini	Mercury	Mercury
Cancer	Moon	Moon
Leo	Sun	Sun
Virgo	Mercury	Mercury / Chiron
Libra	Venus	Venus
Scorpio	Mars	Pluto
Sagittarius	Jupiter	Jupiter
Capricorn	Saturn	Saturn
Aquarius	Saturn	Uranus
Pisces	Jupiter	Neptune

In the traditional method the pattern emanates out of the sun and moon. In Indian mythology it is believed that the sun god and moon goddess sat in heaven. The sun said to Mercury, "As a sign of how fond I am of you, I shall let to you sit at my side. The sun rules its own sign of Leo, so I will give you ruler-ship of Virgo." The moon goddess heard this and said, "I too will seat you (Mercury) beside me and I will give you ruler-ship of Gemini." Then Venus came along and the sun gave the ruler-ship of Libra to Venus, the moon then gave

Taurus to Venus. Mars then followed on, and as a reward was given Scorpio by the sun and Aries by the moon. Jupiter was next in line to be given the rulerships of Sagittarius and Pisces, and finally Saturn ended up the furthest away from the sun having been assigned Capricorn and Aquarius.

Over the last few hundred years a number of new planets have been discovered; namely Uranus, Neptune and Pluto, and these have been given the rulerships of Aquarius, Pisces and Scorpio respectively.

Although this book is a sun sign book, it is worth noting that the transits of your own ruling planet through your sign exert an extra impact, and this is even more so when it makes aspect to your chart.

The Qualities

The qualities underpin many of the characteristics described here, so let us look at them now. Each sign belongs to a quality that may be cardinal, fixed or mutable.

The List of Qualities

Sign	Quality
Aries	Cardinal
Taurus	Fixed
Gemini	Mutable
Cancer	Cardinal
Leo	Fixed
Virgo	Mutable
Libra	Cardinal
Scorpio	Fixed
Sagittarius	Mutable
Capricorn	Cardinal
Aquarius	Fixed
Pisces	Mutable

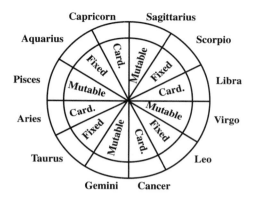

The Qualities of the Signs

The Cardinal Group
Aries, Cancer, Libra, Capricorn

Cardinal types don't let the grass grow under their feet and they are inclined to do what they think best for themselves, their family or their group. They can put themselves out to fit in with others where necessary but they can't leave their own needs too far out in the cold. When the chips are down but they know that they can depend upon themselves. Once they have made their minds up (and this includes the vacillating sign of Libra), they can't be pushed from their path. Cardinal people take advantage of opportunities and they make the most of them, and they can be good leaders as long as they allow others an opinion and an opportunity to use their creativity. One thing they are often good at is motivating and encouraging others but they may then ask or expect too much of others. Despite the strength of this type, their confidence can evaporate and the need the support of a partner or at the very least a couple of good friends.

The Fixed Group
Taurus, Leo, Scorpio, Aquarius

Fixed people try to maintain the status quo, and most prefer a well-ordered life, because too much change makes them uncomfortable. Taureans, Leos and Scorpios need financial security and they fear getting into debt but Aquarians are less concerned about this. A happy relationship and emotional security is important to these people, and they try to work out the problems within a relationship if at all possible rather than giving up at the first hurdle. All fixed sign people are obstinate which may make their life and the lives of those around them difficult in some ways but in others, because when they take on a large task, they do it thoroughly and see it through to a conclusion. Fixed sign people can put up with boredom and repetition if a job requires it, but outside of work they enjoy change and novelty as much as any one else. They have a responsible attitude to life and they take their duties seriously.

The Mutable Group
Gemini, Virgo, Sagittarius, Pisces

Mutable signs need variety and change, and this may take them into careers which ensure that each day is different from the next. Some prefer the kind of job that takes them from one place to another while others travel far afield. Many work in one place but deal with a variety of people or tasks during the course of each day. Mutable sign people may choose unconventional jobs or lifestyles because it is more important for their work to fit in with their beliefs or to fulfil their spiritual needs. They often work in areas that are designed to improve the lot of others than simply for the money or to advance in the conventional sense. There is a streak of independence and unconventionality about all the mutable signs, although this is less obvious in Gemini and Virgo than it is in Sagittarius and Pisces. Many mutable sign types marry when young and start their families early. However, these early relationships all too frequently break up and they may go through a period of experimentation with a variety of partners before settling down with a new partner.

The Genders
Every other sign is masculine or feminine. This has nothing to do with a person's sexuality, but rather more to do with introversion or extroversion. Some astrologers use the terms positive and negative, which are simply different terms for the same thing. The more adventurous, speedy, risk-taking signs belong to the masculine group of Aries, Gemini, Leo, Libra, Sagittarius and Aquarius. The more passive, reactive, thorough and emotional signs belong to the feminine group of Taurus, Cancer, Virgo, Scorpio, Capricorn and Pisces.

Relationships

The ability to get along well with other people is an asset that cannot be overestimated, because practically any activity or area of life involves contact with other human beings. The better you adjust yourself to your family and community, the smoother your path in life will be, but when you become close to other people, the more readily your faults or weaknesses will be tested. The truth is that something is always learned from every encounter; we are all dependent on other individuals to some extent, so one of our tasks in life is to learn how to live with those around us. To do this successfully, we need to understand human nature itself.

We all have similar desires, instincts and urges, although we may express them differently and it helps if we can understand others and ourselves. The sun sign reveals the general temperament of a person, and even without the details that are needed to calculate a full horoscope, knowing about the sun sign can offer a mine of information.

When an astrologer compares the charts of two people to see how they are likely to get along, he pays attention to the combination of all the planets and chart points between the two horoscopes. He looks at how the different parts of the horoscope interact, explains those areas where it will easy for the two people to get on with each other and where there is likely to be a major conflict. Astrologers call this process synastry, and this can provide incredibly detailed information about any type of relationship. Your sun sign describes what is important to you, what you are proud of, where you seek and find success and what you are like. So, even if that is the only information we have about a person, it is often enough to offer a great deal of insight into the way any person approaches or deals with a relationship.

At the start of a romance, both parties have rose tinted glasses planted firmly on the end of their nose. It isn't until the two get to know each other that they discover whether they have mutual interests, whether their views about important issues are compatible and whether there are any serious conflicts of character, habits or ethics. Unless the couple can establish mutual respect, trust and understanding, it is unlikely that the relationship can endure. Any partnership comprises two individuals. Ideally, each should respect the individuality of the other and not allow their own individuality to become a source of conflict. The family unit demands cooperation, respect and mutual consideration, if it is to be successful. By knowing your partner's nature and by gaining an understanding of his or her desires and views, cooperation is far easier to achieve. Sexual compatibility is also important in an intimate partnership. If there are no physical problems on either side, it is possible to overcome initial differences by understanding each person's needs and by good communication.

The stresses on relationships are many and varied. Financial problems, relationships with other family members and differing attitudes to lifestyle can cause untold damage. Sometimes, even when a couple have been together for several years, it can still be possible to improve the relationship by gaining a better understanding about facets of the partner that are puzzling. This knowledge can often save a relationship by dissolving some of the tensions caused by a lack of communication or due to misunderstanding the true nature and motivations of the other person.

Partnerships do not exist in isolation. In a marriage there are parents, children and in-laws to consider, and in today's extended families, there are a variety of other family attachments that can occur. Understanding the motivations and dynamics of others makes it far easier to get along with them.

Children demand a degree of emotional security from their parents. Sometimes the parent needs to be reminded that their child is not simply a clone of himself in the making, but an individual with a distinct personality. Many parents manage their children from a springboard of their own emotions and personalities, motivated by what they want for the child rather than what is most suitable. At times there may be tensions between the parents and child, so by taking care to understand the child, and by laying aside their own prejudices and preferences, parents can establish a long lasting, loving and productive relationship with their offspring.

Understanding the nature of the sun signs may help you to resolve conflicts or help you too find ways in which you can learn to cooperate and live in harmony with your loved-ones. This book seeks to supply you with this information.

Although I have focused on the nuclear family of partner, children, parents, in-laws, grandparents and siblings in this book, you will need to use a little imagination to relate these to the others that are around you. For example, you may feel as loving towards a stepchild or step-parent as if they were your own kin, or you may feel the kind of detachment from a partial relative that you would towards an in-law. Therefore, examine the nature of the relationship in terms of how they feel rather than what they strictly are, and then read through the relevant passages.

Aries

21 March to 20 April
Gender: Masculine
Element: Fire
Quality: Cardinal
Planet: Mars
Symbol: The Ram

Your Character

You are somewhat like your symbol of the Ram because you are willing to fight for what you believe in. You can be gentle but most people see your brash outer side for you tend to keep the softness hidden. You focus on your own ideas and beliefs and you concentrate on getting what you want out of life. You need a mission in life - after all, Aries is named after the God of War! This doesn't necessarily mean that you are a violent or militaristic person, but it does mean that you tackle projects as if they were a mission or a battle plan. You do everything with passion, whether you are actively involved in something or simply a fan of your favorite sporting personality or team - and this is likely to be the underdog side. You are extremely self-willed, so when everyone around you is pulling in one direction, you can pull in another - for all the world like a one-man tug of war team. Sometimes you don't even spot the fact that others are going in a different direction. You can be dogmatic and unwilling to see other people's viewpoints. You are impulsive, independent and you often prefer to go it alone.

Ancient astrological books often been depict Aries as a knight, and this is a very good description of your sign because you charge off into the future. Being idealistic, you see yourself as a modern version of a knight of the Round Table, fighting for something that you believe in. You have a sense of order and discipline and you like things to happen in a logical and orderly manner. You are capable of darting off to do something new but you prefer order, direction and a mission. You are often at the forefront when it comes to helping others - indeed, many Arians get involved in ecological issues, charities or matters of reform.

You can be slightly impractical at times, so you may forget some of the normal everyday issues that people need to concern themselves with, such as taxes and finances. Sometimes you invest money unwisely in schemes that don't work out. When it comes to doing the weekly food shopping, you buy the exciting and interesting foods and only discover when you return home that you have forgotten practical things like bread and milk.

Being excitable, you can become overwrought in the space of a moment and you also find it difficult to stay still. You find it difficult to maintain concentration when a partner wants to discuss feelings or talk about your relationship, so you wander off and find something else to concentrate on rather than sitting down and looking closely at yourself. You become edgy in no time; this can lead to sudden bouts of temper, which do nothing to resolve problems, though if you argue it blows over quickly and you soon forget and settle back down again.

Loyalty means a great deal to you, and when others are disloyal you don't seek revenge, but you never entirely trust the other person again. When others are loyal to you, you follow them to the end of the earth. Treachery is something you cannot understand and if someone stabs you in the back, you pull out of the situation or relationship very quickly. You expect loyalty from your children, so if they abuse your trust it takes work on both sides to repair the damage.

You are extremely loyal to others in all areas of life bar one, which is your fondness for casual romance. The idea of a quick fling with no attachments excites you; not surprisingly, this causes problems once you are in a long-term partnership. If a partner treats you like this, you never forgive them. If you can keep the excitement going in your partnership it will last, but if you have to put up with tension at home or at work, you will suffer from headaches and migraines.

The Aries Child

When young, the Aries child is skinny, but he tends to fill out later. In white races this child's skin needs to be protected from the sun. Aries children (and adults) walk quickly and they need to take care of their feet. They have trouble finding shoes to fit because their feet are either wider or narrower than normal.

This child is full of energy and he finds it hard stay still. He is impatient, inquiring, energetic, and he loves sports or anything that is active, so it is hard to keep up with him. He is very competitive and a sore loser. Being ruled by Mars, he loves militaristic toys, outdoor sports, games of all kinds and also singing and dancing. The Aries child likes to get his own way, so it is important that you don't spoil him. You need to be consistent in your actions, for he will throw a tantrum in the middle of a shop if he decides that he wants a particular type of candy or toy. If you give in, he will exploit this time and again. This tactic needs to be watched because it is not something that he will grow out of.

The Aries child does well at school, especially if the environment is competitive, because he loves to feel as though he is on top. He is bright, but problems can occur if he fails to stay at the top of the class, because he may drop out and search for some other direction to be top of - even if that is the top of the rebellion heap. A young Arian is attracted to the idea of anything that is adventurous or fast, such as becoming a pilot, astronaut or racing driver. This child can make major achievements in the field of sports, sometimes as a team player but also in individual sports, such as athletics. It is wise to encourage this child to work hard at those subjects that he finds difficult, because he needs to qualify in a wide variety of subjects rather than specialize in one subject too early. It is best to ensure that he or she has a good groundwork while still in the process of discovering his particular metier.

Encourage your Aries youngster to join organizations such as scouts as this will allow him to find an outlet for his competitive nature and to instill discipline and self-control. An Aries girl or boy has a natural sense of rhythm, so dancing lessons are an excellent option. He or she also loves music, so it may be worthwhile encouraging them to play an instrument and perhaps to become part of an amateur pop group.

Careers with a strong sense of organization and teamwork will appeal to this child, so he may end up in the armed forces or the police. He may also enjoy the speed and risk involved in the financial market, alternatively anything related to engineering, engines and vehicles will appeal. If he chooses medicine, it will be the drama of surgery or the accident and emergency department that will attract him.

Sex and the Single Aries

Your sign is strongly associated with promiscuous flirtations and short-lived love affairs. Much of this is due to the fact that you act on impulse and don't consider consequences and you also enjoy the flattery that these attractions give to your ego. You may make decisions that you live to regret later. Once you decide on what you want, you steam ahead without stopping to consider the feelings of others. You cannot take no for an answer when you fancy someone because the challenge of a new relationship is so attractive. The niceties of romance don't appeal as much as becoming a partnership soon as possible and this directness can be refreshing.

You can be highly aggravating and it is unfortunate that your partner's anger is exactly what turns you on. When it comes to sex you are easily aroused. Although you might not be as imaginative as some, you're open-minded and you have passion to spare - and you can be very demanding. Subtlety and quietness aren't on your agenda when it comes to sex. Your enthusiasm is as apparent and you want to keep the passion going.

Marriage and Partnership

Though you're more than able to supply plenty of excitement and action, you are not so good at offering security and stability. However, once you decide that a relationship is for keeps you're capable of being scrupulously faithful, but there is always the risk of wandering if your needs aren't met. Most Arians want a storybook romance with the realities of life kept at a distance, and the last thing they want is to feel trapped. You hope to receive the same level of devotion that you give, and any indiscretions of your partner's part are hard to forgive. Whatever your gender, love is based on sharing and equal rights. An Aries is the first to make up after any quarrel, mainly because he wants to stay in charge. So long as passion and romance are kept alive, marriage can last a long time. If things go wrong, you will put plenty of energy into repairing the relationship before deciding to move on, and you're unlikely to start a new relationship before ending the old.

With a Fire Sign Partner

Both of you are passionate, so the sparks fly when you got together! The relationship starts up spontaneously and quickly, and while this is a very good combination, occasionally it can be too fiery and you may end up fighting. It is important that you pull together and that each of you learns to control your tempestuous natures. It is also important to work out who is responsible for which areas of family life.

Aries/Aries

There may be an initial attraction but interest can wane quickly as you are both competitive and neither of you shrink from an argument.

Aries/Leo

This is an explosive combination with a lot of potential for clashes, unless one of you can learn to compromise. This can turn into an enjoyable short-term fling.

Aries/Sagittarius

Both are enthusiastic and ready to throw yourselves into the relationship with complete abandon, but the Sagittarian desire for freedom may cause problems if you begin to take the affair too seriously. Having said this, it is a combination that has the potential to work.

With an Earth Sign Partner

Your abundant energy makes a nice blend with the practicality of earth, although the earth sign partner can find you too pushy at times. Earth sign people are obstinate but reliable, so you can expect the loyalty that you crave, but you will need to work at creating or maintaining the excitement.

Aries/Taurus

You want to leap right in while Taurus is still considering the advantages of the affair, so sometimes the Taurean's reactions may be too slow for romantic involvement.

Aries/Virgo

You can find Virgo too critical and Virgo doesn't like to be rushed into things, so this is a difficult combination.

Aries/Capricorn

It is not easy to mix your fire and spontaneity with Capricorn's practicality and stability, but occasionally this combination surprises everyone by emerging as a serious relationship.

With an Air Sign Partner

Fire and air is a volatile mixture, but in a relationship it works very well, because the air sign subject offers encouragement and enthusiasm.

Air signs like to think things through before embarking on them and this curtails your instantaneous attitude to life. But once you both agree on an idea or a project you can work well together.

Aries/Gemini

This combination might never get off the ground as Gemini spends time analyzing and rationalizing, and this can dampen your initial enthusiasm.

Aries/Libra

You demand a level of intensity that Libra dislikes and Libra wants more commitment and solid romance than you may be willing to supply, but this one can work well if you are ready to settle down.

Aries/Aquarius

You want to leap in head first while Aquarius is still considering the consequences, so it is an unlikely combination; however, there is a level of intellectual respect and sensuality that can make this work.

With a Water Sign Partner

This partnership works well in a traditional relationship, if you are a man and a breadwinner and the water sign partner is a woman and a homemaker, but as this is not often the case these days, it can be fraught with problems. Water signs require constant reassurance and approval from their partners, so you might find this lover's dependency too restrictive. You would need to adapt to ensure that you provide the comfort and security that a water partner needs.

Aries/Cancer

This can be a volatile combination, but Cancer appreciates your talent for taking the initiative and you appreciate the differences in nature. You may become bored with Cancer's sensitivity and Cancer might ask for more commitment than you are willing to give.

Aries/Scorpio

A highly charged combination, but Scorpio is unlikely to enjoy your habit of teasing and your lack of sensitivity and Scorpio may end up feeling resentful and angry. Though difficult in the long term it could be an exciting short-lived affair.

Aries/Pisces

Piscean subtlety is completely alien to your direct method of approach, so this is an unlikely combination.

Starting a Family

If you are an Aries man, you may feel under pressure to prove your virility by reproducing as soon as possible. If you are an Aries woman, you won't spend much time contemplating pregnancy, but when you fall pregnant you will be full of enthusiasm and you will hardly be able to wait until the little one arrives. You will find it frustrating to slow down during pregnancy and to be unable to do everything that you did before, or to do it all at top speed. The medical profession won't be able to boss you around during pregnancy because you are more than capable of standing up for yourself. When it comes to the actual moment of giving birth you tend to regard it as a battle to be won at all costs, so relaxation and meditation techniques before the event will help you to go with the flow.

As an Aries parent, you love to involve yourself in your child's education. You are likely to become active in a parent-teacher committee and you can be counted on to be present at sports events, cheering your child on - if not actually taking part yourself. You strive for status and success yourself and you need to guard against doing this through your children, because you must give your children space and allow them to develop in their own ways. Yours is a childlike sign, which pays off when you become involved with your children, sharing in their games and teaming up against outsiders.

With a Fire Sign Child

You share a love of sport and your enjoyment of the outdoor life. You probably even enjoy the same kind of music. You will need to constantly encourage your fire sign child and it will be necessary to lay down some ground rules and discipline from an early age. The chances are that you will fall out once the child reaches his teens, and there may be furious arguments at that time.

With an Earth Sign Child

You will encourage your this child to work that little bit harder than he wants to do, and you will do what you can to improve his self-confidence. You will enliven him but you can't expect him to do things at the same pace as you. He won't share your interests, and he may prefer to concentrate on music or practical subjects.

With an Air Sign Child

This is a difficult relationship, as you will be frustrated by your child's tendency to change his interests at a moment's notice. This child will not even support the same soccer or baseball team for more then two years in a row. His enthusiasm for life will please you but his lack of concentration will aggravate you. You will get along well enough intellectually but there will be heated arguments until he discovers what he wants to be and settles into a career.

With a Water Sign Child

This is not an easy mix. You will find this child clinging and dependent and you will wonder if he will ever stand on his own two feet. Having said this, you will enjoy the attention that this child gives you.

Adult Relationships

The next section talks about your relationships with parents and parental figures once you yourself are an adult.

With a Fire Sign Parent

This is a strong combination because you share similar ideals but when you disagree there can be major conflict. You both need to work hard to make a success of this relationship. You have a similar do-or-die attitude that succeeds when you pull together but the sparks fly when you don't.

With an Earth Sign Parent

This is generally a very good combination, because earth sign parents often give practical help and understanding. You can't be what they want or follow their practical and sustained attitude to life, but no matter how much they disapprove of your chosen path in life they will always be there for you.

With an Air Sign Parent

Your parents will support your actions and your choice of pathway in life even if they don't always agree with you. At times you'll wish they could offer more practical help and this may make you feel quite alone at times.

With a Water Sign Parent

This is not the best mix, as your parents' over-emotional reaction to life will puzzle you; they may also want more affection from you than you can give. Whatever happens, they will always be there with support when you need it. You will be irritated by their habit of bring up past arguments and problems - water sign memories are long and often unforgiving.

In-laws and Similar relationships

This section deals with your relationships with adults who are attached to you in some way but not related to you by blood.

With Fire Sign In-laws

While your interests, ideas and personalities are similar, this doesn't always make for a very good combination. The in-laws are as competitive as you are, and they will expect you to achieve their standards of housekeeping or their level of success in a career. Differences in opinion will be a major source of conflict.

With Earth Sign In-laws

Your in-laws want to involve themselves in your life whereas you prefer to go it alone, but there will be times when you will find yourself grateful for their help, so try not to resist them too much. They will be willing to help out when you have financial problems, but they will dislike your impractical attitude and your impetuousness.

They may also be a little jealous of your talents and abilities, but you acknowledge the fact that they are more astute about financial matters, and it is no use trying to compete with their cordon bleu cooking skills!

With Air Sign In-laws

Avoid playing word games with these people, as they will win every time. If your partner gives up a career or educational aspirations for you they will blame you and never forgive you. This will be the case even if you are successful, as this will add envy of your exciting lifestyle to the already volatile mixture.

With Water Sign In-laws

These in-laws will not hesitate to invade your home, tidy up your house, arrange your life and give you the impression that your partner has never really left home. On the positive side, they are always available for baby-sitting when you feel like a night out.

Aries Grandchildren

You are extremely generous and great fun and you will happily play alongside the youngsters and take them out to fetes, trips and even vacations - you will even arrange parties for your grandchildren. The chances are that you have a life of your own, so you are not around all the time and the children will find your company an exciting treat and a pleasant change.

With Siblings

As a child you competed fiercely with your brothers, sisters and others in your family but you also loved them fiercely. If an outsider attacked any one of your siblings you would have gone after them with all guns blazing. You fought for your share (perhaps the lion's share) of your parents' attention. A quieter or more introspective brother or sister may have found your noisy, active nature irritating but they would have loved your sunny, enthusiastic and optimistic outlook on life. You remain reasonably close in adult life.

Choosing a Pet

You prefer active pets and you can't see the point of very small creatures such as goldfish or hamsters, so you enjoy a lively dog. Greyhounds and working dogs of all kinds may suit you as well.

Your Vehicle

You like excitement and change, so you go for a different kind of vehicle every time you buy one. You love to be in control but you also enjoy a challenge, so you may prefer a manual transmission to an automatic. You look for engine power rather than auto-dipping mirrors or other comforts or extras and you are so into vehicles and engines that you may service and tune your car yourself. You get more speeding tickets than most of the other signs.

Taurus

21 April to 21 May
Gender: Feminine
Element: Earth
Quality: Fixed
Planet: Venus
Symbol: The Bull

Your Character

Like your symbol the Bull, you are loyal, steadfast, dependable, determined and often immovable. Emotional and material security is of paramount importance to you, so it is vital for you to feel safe and secure and to protect your own environment. Your fixed opinions mean that you sometimes find it difficult to see things from another person's point of view. You find it very difficult to change and adapt, which means that you can miss out on opportunities that would bring benefits. You are a strong-willed person and you can be obstinate.

Taurus is ruled by the planet, Venus, which endows a peaceful and serene energy to those born under this sign, so you prefer to live in peace. Venus is a planet of financial luck, which is very useful if you enter a career in finance. Venus also endows you with an appreciation of beauty, art and music - and you may have an artistic streak. Many dancers and musicians share your sign but as you are not keen on taking risks, you probably keep your artistic abilities as a hobby rather than attempting to make a living from them. However, if you do make a career in this area you are likely to remain in it and to be successful.

Taurus is a very sensual sign, so you really enjoy all the physical pleasures in life. As well as music and art, you are likely to enjoy eating and drinking and you may well be an excellent cook, especially when you can bring creativity and imagination into your cooking. This means that you may have a battle to keep from becoming overweight.

You can be very financially astute and will invest your money wisely. When you do spend money, you are likely to be drawn to buying beautiful paintings or objects that will not only make your environment more beautiful, but may also appreciate in value. Alternatively, you may spend money on improving your house, thus increasing its value. You can save for a rainy day and you prefer to save for something you want to buy, although you can wait so long that when you decide to make a purchase, the bargain you wanted has gone. My Taurean mother used to complain about the size of the kitchen and how it lacked the facilities that she could have done with. Then, after waiting for many years she eventually got the kitchen she wanted, which included a cooker with massive twin ovens and eight rings and a dishwasher. Unfortunately by the time she got it, my sister, two brothers and myself had long moved out, so now it only occasionally gets used at full capacity! As for the dishwasher - it was four months before it ever got used, as she didn't have enough dishes to warrant using it!

Your family is very important to you. You need to be part of a close-knit family and you will do anything to protect them if possible. If a relationship turns sour and there are too many arguments and fights to keep things together, you will do anything you can to keep your possessions. You will also fight for custody of your children. Taurean divorces can be quite nasty! One Taurean male I know, fought for and got custody of his daughter; he brought her up on his own, and he was also the first man in Britain to receive maintenance from his wife!

You are a hard worker but you can be a bit of a plodder, so it may take a while for you to reach your potential. Combined with your need for security and dislike of taking risks, this may restrict some of your career opportunities. Being good with finances, careers such as banking, insurance and accountancy could be suitable for you. Artistic careers are also possibilities, and you can run an antiques shop - as long as you are willing to sell the things that you collect. The more practical Taurean may be well suited to a career in building. Certainly as an earth sign you would make an excellent farmer or gardener.

Relationships are very important to you and you want them to be permanent. You are a very stable and loyal person and you prefer your courtship to follow a traditional route. Even in love, you approach things in a practical way - although you can be romantic, and you like to show your affection by showering your lover with gifts. In forming new relationships, you may miss opportunities because you don't always notice when someone is attracted to you.

You can be very possessive in a relationship (possibly even overpossessive), and you can aggravate your partner by wanting to know where they are all the time. However, you are generally easygoing, patient and slow to anger, but when you do get annoyed you can be like the bull in the china shop! Female Taureans are usually charming and beautiful in a sensual way, often with large round eyes. They are very loyal in relationships and they want to please.

The Taurus Child

The Taurus child can be obstinate and fixed in his ways so it is worth teaching him to become more adaptable, as long as you can do so without appearing to oppose him. He may be keen on music and he could be a good singer. If music isn't his thing, then art, hairdressing, gardening, design or cooking may interest him. This child likes to collect things, so he may have many furry toys, toy automobiles or even a pile of ancient comics. Your Taurus child can be lazy so it is important to push and cajole him at times, particularly where education is concerned. At school you will find that he is likely to shine in arts and crafts subjects but he will struggle with scientific ones, although he will be good at mathematics. He is not likely to be keen on sports but he will be extremely sociable and he should be quite popular.

Taurean children usually want to be well dressed, so yours may pay a good deal of attention to clothes and fashion. He can be quiet, so you need to ensure he doesn't become too solitary. He won't always tell you what's going on in his mind.

Sex and the Single Taurean

You are torn between loving and needing plenty of sex and being happier in a permanent relationship. This means that you are bound to experiment a little while young, but you soon start to look for a long-term venture. You need plenty of affection, though you can be a bit on the lazy side when it comes to seeking it. Your feelings are deep and strong but you're not always that demonstrative, although sex has to be a combination of sensation and affection. You take things slowly because pleasure is more important than excitement as far as you're concerned. You're very sensual, you have plenty of staying power and you like to take your time. Lots of stroking, hugs and kisses are always part of your sexual experience. You are pretty conventional with no great wish to experiment and so you are not difficult to satisfy.

Marriage and Partnership

It make take you a while before you realize when you've found the right relationship - but once that decision is made you'll stick with it come what may. Buying a house and furnishing it is one of the first things on your mind - because for you, tomorrow is what matters and you're prepared to delay having fun in the present in favor of a secure future.

Your relationships are not always the most exciting because you prefer contentment. A combination of common sense, coupled with a strong desire to live in harmony means that your relationship is likely to be more stable than those of others. You are loyal and steadfast and therefore extremely unlikely to be unfaithful. Being practical and home loving, you're more than happy to do your fair share around the house.

You don't often get angry but when your temper is aroused the results can be quite frightening. You will stay around even when things get rough, because you believe that patience will solve your problems. If your relationship does break down, it can take you a very long time to get over it.

With a Fire Sign Partner

As long as your fire sign partner is relatively quiet and home loving, this can work. Another possibility is the kind of traditional marriage where the fire sign partner brings home the bacon and you cook it. This combination has more chance of succeeding later in life than when you and your lover are both young.

Taurus/Aries

Aries wants to leap right in while you are still thinking about whether you want a relationship or not. You share a fondness for sex but your desire for a stable home life may be too mundane for Aries.

Taurus/Leo

You both love family life and you will both adore your children. You also share artistic or creative interests, and you may even enjoy playing musical instruments together. You are both rather stubborn though, so arguments are likely.

Taurus/Sagittarius

This can work with the quieter type of Sagittarian, but if you try to form a relationship with the kind who can't bear the idea of being tied down or living in one place, this one will not even begin to get off the ground.

With an Earth Sign Partner

Earth sign people have a similar outlook to you and they will share the same interests, so this should work well. Outsiders will view your choice of lifestyle as a little dull, but as long as you and your lover are happy, so what?

Taurus/Taurus

This is a satisfactory relationship as you are both family people who want a quite but comfortable lifestyle. You share an interest in travel, children, pets, your home and creative or artistic ventures. You also leave each other alone to get on with things, so all in all this should be a happy relationship.

Taurus/Virgo

The two of you can develop warmth between you and you are likely to have confidence in one another. This could well be a sensual and happy long-term relationship.

Taurus/Capricorn

Capricorn is ambitious, and while you also like money and the good things of life, you may have to leave it to your partner to provide the bulk of this. There is plenty of compatibility here, so this one should work well.

With an Air Sign Partner

You share an interest in making an attractive home, but you may be more interested in family life than your partner. Mentally, you are on such different wavelengths that it is hard to see this standing the test of time, especially if your partner has a roving eye.

Taurus/Gemini

There is so little common ground between the two of you that a romance is extremely unlikely.

Taurus/Libra

There are some similarities here as you are both artistic and musical, and you are also both keen on domestic matters such as cooking and gardening. As long as you take care of the family and allow Libra some space, this can work - and it can be a successful sexual union.

Taurus/Aquarius

About the only things you have in common are fixed opinions and obstinacy. You are on such different wavelengths and your attitudes to home and family life are so opposed, that it is hard to see this working. Aquarius is unlikely to give you the emotional security and affection that you crave.

With a Water Sign Partner

This combination can work because you both need emotional security. Your water sign lover's moodiness may irritate you but otherwise you have plenty in common. If your partner is the type who needs romance and excitement, he may eventually become bored with you and start to stray.

Taurus/Cancer

This can be a nurturing and comfortable relationship for both of you, and it is potentially long lasting.

Taurus/Scorpio

This is likely to be a passionate relationship, but tempers will occasionally flare. As long as neither of you try to dominate the other or keep the other short of money, this can turn into a fairly successful long-term partnership.

Taurus/Pisces

An initial attraction is likely as you may share artistic, musical and creative interests, although sooner or later, your lover's lack of practicality will irritate you. You may find his intense interest in psychic or spiritual matters totally incomprehensible.

Starting a Family

As a Taurean, you'll spend as much time and money as you can afford to make sure that the new arrival's life is wonderful. Although you're certainly capable of showing the affection that a young child needs you may have to remind yourself that money really can't buy love. Your baby will appreciate a cuddle from you far more than from a giant teddy bear! You may view your child as a possession rather than an independent person with his or her own preferences and there is bound to be some conflict when he is older and he refuses to do things your way.

As a Taurus woman, the chances are that you prepare everything you need shortly after you become pregnant. You'll have a freshly decorated nursery and you will try to ensure that the experience of pregnancy is as comfortable as possible. You will be keen to indulge yourself - lounging on the sofa, munching a few chocolates and reserving your energy for when you really need it. It's unlikely that you'll panic at any stage because your sensible approach means that you take things as they come, and you are perfectly happy to enjoy the most sensual experience of your life.

With a Fire Sign Child

Your child will appreciate the stable upbringing that you give him but sooner or later he is bound to rebel against your rather fixed opinions, so it is important that you learn to see things from his point of view and to be willing to adapt. Fire sign children are great achievers, so this child will give you something to be proud of.

With an Earth Sign Child

This combination works well until you disagree with each other, because with two such strong-willed personalities there are bound to be a few clashes, so you will both need to compromise a little. It will be easy for you to understand this child and to offer him the emotional security that he needs.

With an Air Sign Child

This is not an easy combination because you are likely to be too staid and serious for him and he can be too flippant and too ready to drop one interest in favor of a new one for your taste. On a positive note, you will provide security and your child will usually take your advice when he needs it.

With a Water Sign Child

This is a good combination, as you can provide each other with the security you need. This child may irritate you at times, because he will want to stay indoors while you are keen for him to get out and about and to explore the countryside. You may need to encourage him to be more active and sporty. He will also need encouragement if he is to do well at school.

Adult Relationships

This section deals with your feelings about parents or those who you see as parent figures.

With a Fire Sign Parent

These parents might be frustrated by your apparent slowness when young, but you will take them by surprise later in life by become more successful than they would have imagined. These parents will appreciate your home-loving ways and they will be happy to come round for a meal and to enjoy the peace and beauty that is to be found in your home. Social occasions are likely to be pleasant and agreeable.

With an Earth Sign Parent

This is potentially a good match as you share the same basic personality and a similar fondness for security.

Disagreements are possible due to the fact that you are both stubborn, so this is one of those relationships that either works well or not at all. You will keep in touch with these parents.

With an Air Sign Parent

It is just as well that you like being the king or queen of your own castle, because these parents will not wish to interfere in your home life. They may criticize your lack of achievement at work or your paucity of outside interests, but you won't listen to them, so it doesn't matter.

With a Water Sign Parent

Your outlook is similar in many ways, although your parents will be less practical than you are. They will be ready to help out with baby-sitting and you can call on them for help when you need a hand with jobs around the home.

In-laws and Similar Relationships

You have a live and let live towards those who are not related to you by ties of blood, so unless they seek to criticize or interfere, this relationship should be reasonably good.

With Fire Sign In-laws

These relatives will not understand your need for financial security but they will enjoy socializing with you.

With Earth Sign In-laws

You share common sense and a practical attitude to life, so you should get on very well together.

With Air Sign In-laws

These in-laws will be amusing and friendly, so you will enjoy their company on a social level, but there is not enough in common between you for you to become close friends.

With Water Sign In-laws

This should be an easy relationship, as you are all home loving and family minded. You will enjoy getting together for a barbecue or the occasional family outing. Their bouts of moodiness may irritate you and if they make unpleasant remarks, you will not be able to keep your temper.

Grandchildren

This is where your patience really comes into its own, as you can take the kids off their parents' hands and amuse them for hours. If your grandchildren are heavily into sports, you will be there to cheer them on, although you probably won't want to play active games with them.

With Siblings

As long as your brothers and sisters are pleasant to you, you will be able to maintain a relationship with them throughout life. If they are critical or unpleasant, you will have as little to do with them as possible.

Choosing a Pet

Almost any pet will suit you and it is unlikely that you will go through life without an animal. You would particularly enjoy the company of a playful and pretty cat.

Your Vehicle

Your automobile must be impressive and attractive, but also fuel-efficient, as you don't like to waste money.

Gemini

22 May to 21 June
Gender: Masculine
Element: Air
Quality: Mutable
Planet: Mercury
Symbol: The Twins

Your Character

Gemini people are always quick to tell me that they are double sided or that they have a split personality. Perhaps you are simply more conscious of your inner and outer personality than members of other signs are. Your sign is that of the twins, so you can vacillate a little at times.

You enjoy conversation and contact with people, and you love to have your mind stimulated. Being quick to become bored, you can lose interest in a person or a particular task and to quickly move on to something different. You are very flexible in your attitude and quick to look at new things and new ideas, so much so that it is sometimes difficult for you to keep your mind on one thing without wanting to veer off and look at something else. Being somewhat gossipy, you like to keep in touch with others and to remain up to date. You are interested in gadgets, literature and anything that expands the mind. It is easy for you to understand other points of view and this makes you very good at situations where it is important to look at both sides of an argument.

You love to read, especially the kind of fiction that allows you to escape the humdrum world. Some of you read so much that you end up writing (sometimes because you feel that you can do better than others). However novel writing takes too long, so many of you end up in journalism and broadcasting where you don't need to concentrate on one subject for too long.

You love spending money on clothes so you appreciate a partner who earns good money. If you are the one who earns the money, you are not likely to be stingy and you will ensure that all your family members are properly looked after. One thing for sure is that you cannot take on a sickly partner or one who harps on about health matters because you are not the world's best nurse and your patience soon wears thin. Some Geminis are real miseries who moan and complain about their lot in life. However, the chances are that you are not like this, and that the flexibility of your nature allows you to roll with the punches. If you have to change your job, you will worry until you settle into the new one, but you will also enjoy the opportunity that a new job offers for making new friends.

The Gemini Child

This child picks up things quickly and he is bright, but he can easily drift from one subject to another. He needs encouragement in order to fulfil his true potential, but if he does so, he will go to the top in his chosen career. He will need no encouragement to read, and he will also enjoy making or fixing things. Light sports, such as tennis and badminton will appeal to him.

An ideal career is journalism, but this child would make a good teacher, writer or lawyer, or he may drift towards the world of advertising where he can use words and ideas in short bursts. His enthusiasm for talking to other people makes him a good sales person, but he can also find a niche in the travel trade. He may end up doing two part-time jobs.

Sex and the Single Gemini

Like all the air signs, you love the idea of an exiting affair with no strings attached and you may choose a fire sign for this kind of liaison. You bore quickly and you need variety. It can be hard to for concentrate on the same partner for long as don't have a lot of staying power. It is said that Gemini will try anything once except monogamy! It is not that you're immoral - it is just that the theoretical ideal you aim towards can change according to your mood of the moment. A need for constant stimulation makes it possible for you to carry on two love affairs simultaneously and many Geminis run a marriage in the background while stopping off for brief flings, or even a long-term romance on the side.

This need for stimulation means that you enjoy playing games, and when it comes to sex you can be calculating. You enjoy the bizarre and weird and you are an expert at lying and faking. Fantasy is often of more interest to you than reality and you may enjoy pornography and sex toys. Sex games and mirrors in the bedroom also appeal. Your sign is strongly associated with sexual perversions but for most it is simply a case of being more adventurous than most.

Marriage and Partnership

Your home is wherever you happen to be, so you don't worry too much about decor and so forth. You like the idea of someone being around, but don't want to be leaned on too much, because there is a part of you that you like to keep to yourself and not share with anyone. It is likely that you will marry when young, but this may not last, so more than one marriage is a possibility for you.

You are capable of being a terrible flirt, but if faith is placed in you then you are less likely to be dishonest. Mental harmony is of paramount importance if a relationship is to last the distance. Life is never boring with you and you enjoy a lively social life outside the home. Housework bores you rigid - there are so many more interesting things to do.

You are amazingly supportive to a good partner, and you will even put up with a less good one if the sex and money are there when you need them. As long as your life together offers variety and your job encompasses a variety of tasks, you can stick with jobs and partners for long periods of time.

Oddly enough for someone who is so interested in the outside world, you are also extremely interested in your children. When they leave home, you will always keep in touch with them and be there for them when they need you.

With Fire Sign Partner

This starts out as an exciting relationship with plenty of fun and laughter, but you can become bored and your tendency to moan and worry about everything will drive your partner nuts. You would both have to work hard to make it last.

Gemini/Aries

Your tendency to analyze and rationalize everything is alien to Aries, and your habit of worrying about things that may never happen will annoy your lover, but this combination can work if Aries brings in the money and lets you spend it.

Gemini/Leo

You soon learn to manipulate Leo, and you may not be the constant and loyal companion that Leo requires.

Gemini/Sagittarius

Your similarities make you good friends and your shared interest in variety offers plenty of excitement. Neither of you is consistent or wants to give your all to a marriage, so it may be short lived.

With an Earth Sign Partner

This is a difficult blend, as you can find an earth sign partner dull and far too security conscious, but this lover offers a certain amount of stability, and that can be an advantage in the long run.

Gemini/Taurus

There is so little common ground between you that a long-term romance is extremely unlikely.

Gemini/Virgo

You cannot offer Virgo the security he needs, so after the initial magnetic attraction has worn off, Virgo may decide to wave goodbye.

Gemini/Capricorn

Capricorn may overwhelm you with his or her need for commitment, especially when you are only hoping for a lighthearted, uncomplicated affair.

With an Air Sign Partner

This is a good blend due to the similarity in your natures, but you may not share the same passions and interests, so you could find yourselves drifting apart after a while. This one seems to work out better for those who are a little older, and who have had other experiences of life and love.

Gemini/Gemini
Lots of excitement is on offer but it's more likely that this relationship never reaches the stage of romance as so much of this is lived in your heads.

Gemini/Libra
A cerebral combination with sex added. You could both give flirting lessons and neither of you will be particularly interested in being faithful.

Gemini/Aquarius
You are both independent and you both need space. If you have interests in common and careers of your own, this can turn into a successful relationship.

With a Water Sign Partner
Water sign partners are emotional while you are rational so you may never understand how they come to their conclusions or what they are feeling. You may find them heavy going due to their constant need for reassurance, so this does not make this the best match in the world.

Gemini/Cancer
Your tendency to flit about can upset the Cancer's need for stability, so this is unlikely to work.

Gemini/Scorpio
You find it hard to get to grips with Scorpio's intensity and Scorpio finds you superficial. There could be a mutual

fascination but a lack of any understanding makes it unlikely to go far. You may find that the Scorpio person unnerves you in some way.

Gemini/Pisces
Whereas you live in your head, Pisces dwells in the world of feeling. It would be difficult for you to find enough common ground.

Starting a Family
Starting a family is a whole new challenge to you. As soon as the decision is made, you gather all the information you need, buy the books and watch the videos. As a Gemini woman, you become a mine of information on pregnancy and childbirth as soon as you know you're about to greet a new member of the family. You ask everyone you know what it was like for them and you analyze every possible permutation of how your pregnancy can go and the type of birth. Antenatal groups were designed for people like you where the exchange of ideas and experiences can make your pregnancy as mentally stimulating as it is physically. When the moment finally arrives you want it all to be over as quickly as possible - after all, here is someone new to meet, and you want to meet them now.

The early days of a new baby may be a little disappointing as the routine of caring for them cannot offer the mental stimulation you so badly need. But you're more than prepared to go down on your hands and knees, pull silly faces or do whatever it takes to entertain the little one. Better than anyone, you know the importance of keeping a small child's brain stimulated.

With a Fire Sign Child

The quickness of this child's mind and his many interests make this a comfortable combination, but you may want to your child to take an interest in a wider range of subjects than he feels that he can handle. When this youngster gets older, you will be reasonably happy with anything he chooses to do with his life, even if his choices are quite different from yours.

With an Earth Sign Child

You will find this child's obstinacy infuriating and he may need more constancy and security than you are willing to give, while your inconsistency will unnerve this child. However, you will appreciate his practical approach and you will soon engage his help in practical problems, and you may eventually lean on this child's strength more than is healthy.

With an Air Sign Child

Communication is easy and you will be happy to provide books, a computer, trips to places of interest and plenty of mental stimulation. You may wish to share hobbies but you both tend to lose interest in them after a while. Your child will make friends easily and then drop them quickly. The same inconsistency will apply to jobs and relationships until they reach true maturity.

With a Water Sign Child

Your water element child will need plenty of love and understanding and your independence and occasional remoteness will confuse and worry your child. He needs to know that he can hold your attention for more than just a few minutes at a time. When he is older, you may try to prevent him from committing to a relationship at too young an age.

Adult Relationships
Let us now look at how you get on with your own parents or the parental figures in your own adult life.

With a Fire Sign Parent
They will want you to put more effort and enthusiasm into tasks than you care for, but when you do something that they approve of they will help you as much as they can. This parent will love you deeply and you will share several interests and a lot of laughter.

With an Earth Sign Parent
This is not the easiest of mixes because an earth parent would prefer you to have a more controlled and static lifestyle than you would like, but this parent will be ready with practical support whenever you need it. This parent will offer unwanted advice and opinions but they will support you in anything that you decide to do.

With an Air Sign Parent
This is a comfortable relationship because you share the same element, and while you can be great friends, you cannot rely on each other in any practical way. This is an excellent relationship for shared business matters because you share a similar kind of imaginative flair. One thing for sure is that you will chat to each other regularly and you will enjoy shopping expeditions or socializing together.

With a Water Sign Parent
These parents will want to monopolize you and be involved in your family life, and this will put a lot of emotional pressure on you. You will become impatient with them, but you won't want to admit this.

In-laws and Similar Relationships
These detached relationships can suit you well, providing that the in-laws are neither critical nor interfering. You could become friendly and sociable towards your in-laws.

With Fire Sign In-laws
This is quite a good combination, as they won't want to interfere with the way you do things and they will respect you for your enthusiasm. You will get on well together even if you don't always agree with their attitudes.

With Earth Sign In-laws
You can call upon these in-laws for practical help, but they may irritate you by trying to tell you how to run your home or live your life.

With Air Sign In-laws
You have similar interests and you would enjoy going off on adventurous holidays or playing sports together. As long as you are on each other's wavelength, you can enjoy each other's company.

With Water Sign In-laws
Although you share many of their ideals, this is a tough one. They won't want to let you out of their sight because they want to be involved in your household and to become part of your family. It is important to make sure that you and your partner have your own life to lead. Let them know that you want them around sometimes, but not so much that they cramp your social life or make your weekends monotonous.

Grandchildren

You will adore your grandchildren when they are babies, but your relationship will really bloom when they are old enough to play with. The new generation's games and toys will absolutely fascinate you, and your children will be only too happy to leave you and the grandchildren together to play on the computer and learn together.

With Siblings

You probably have quite a good relationship with brothers and sisters even in childhood and you become even closer to them in adulthood. You will never live in any relative's pocket or get under their feet, but you like to keep in touch and to meet up. The chances are that in adult life, you get on far better with your siblings than you do your with your parents.

Choosing a Pet

Many of you are real softies when it comes to animals, and you are bound to have at least one. I have known some Geminis who have a many pets, but for the most part this is too much like hard work. You like cats and dogs.

Your Vehicle

You cannot live without a car because the thought of not being mobile suffocates you. It is hard for you to work out exactly what kind of vehicle you want because you are attracted to the idea of a speedy sporty model as well as something that will carry ten people. Perhaps two cars would suit your double-sided personality? One thing for sure is that you do more mileage than many of the other signs, so you need something that is reliable - but also interesting.

Cancer

22 June to 23 July
Gender: Feminine
Element: Water
Quality: Cardinal
Planet: The Moon
Symbol: The Crab

Your Character

Like your symbol, the Crab, when you feel yourself under attack, you hide inside your shell and scuttle away into a corner - but you can defend yourself stoutly and you will do anything to protect your family from attack. You project a tough image, which is different from your inner personality, and you can be prone to bouts of depression and self-doubt. Security is very important because you need to feel financially and emotionally safe, which means that you are probably most suited to life in a traditional family environment. If someone around you needs help, you may jump in quickly and find yourself being used by them. It is best to consider the facts behind any sob stories that you hear before wading in financially or in any other way.

You can be quite shrewd and clever in business matters, but you have to guard against becoming so enthusiastic about a venture that you dive in without checking it out and without considering the potential downside. A strange kind of sloppiness can take you over, so that you lose money or opportunities that others would not miss. Your fear of financial insecurity can make you penny-pinching, but a sudden change of mood can turn you into a kind of one-man social security agency. Sometimes your moods take you over to the extent that you lose all sense of proportion. The same goes for matters of the heart, because you endow the object of your desire with all kinds of noble attributes and you can make excuses for all kinds of poor behavior.

You can be very attached to the past and you find it difficult to shrug off past hurts and to move on, and this can be wearing on those around you. However, you also have great courage and determination and you can overcome difficulties that would defeat others. You will also fight hard for any member of your family who needs help, and you even take on hopeless cases within your own family.

The Cancer Child

As a baby, this child is very placid and he should sleep through the night from a very early age. This youngster needs constant reassurance and love, and he shouldn't require harsh discipline because he wants to win the approval of his parents, teachers and others and he hates to be told off or made to feel ashamed. Being modest and shy, he is not quick to make friends outside the family and if he has one or two unpleasant experiences with friends, he won't bother to make any new ones. The Cancerian child is often the oldest in the family or the one who cares for the younger ones. Some of these children are fearful and even phobic at times, due to their deep-rooted feelings of insecurity. It is a good idea to keep films and television programs about war and disaster away from this child.

From the start, this child will show a great affinity for pets and animals and he may even decide at an early age on a career that involves working with animals. The Cancer child is a born nurturer so he will aim for such careers as nursing, caring for children, teaching and social work. While at school, he will show an interest in history and English literature and many of these children go on to become historians and archaeologists.

Sex and the Single Cancerian

Frankly, there isn't likely to be much of this, because you are not suited to flings or short-lived affairs. You are happy to date and you can be extremely flirtatious but you simply cannot cope with a physical relationship that has no real meaning or depth because you prefer to be part of a family.

Marriage and Partnership

You are most suited to the kind of deep and meaningful relationship that has the potential of lasting a lifetime. Even your friendships are serious and long-term. Being romantic, you want to love, trust and possess the object of your desire. You need to feel special to one person and you are unlikely to be promiscuous. In matters of love, you are tender and affectionate. Fearing rejection, you take things slowly, but if a relationship looks as if it will work, you cannot hide your true feelings for long. You may be a little moody at times, but are capable of great tenacity and faithfulness and you are willing to sacrifice your own needs in return for affection. You don't take criticism from a partner lightly though, and you fear ridicule.

Sex is part of a relationship and you don't get excited about strange practices or making love in strange places, because the truth is that you feel most comfortable in your own bed. You're straightforward in your approach and you are a considerate lover, but once you get started you sometimes find it difficult to stop. It is unlikely that you would do anything without consulting your partner. Promiscuity doesn't interest you and you will do all in your power to ensure that your lover doesn't stray. Even though you may fancy a fling, once this starts your heart and feelings soon become engaged so that even your flings tend to last for years.

Once you have settled into a relationship your desire for security and your natural ability to handle life and domestic matters ensures that you cope with this very well and you ensure that the bills are paid on time. You want the best quality in anything so the contents of your home are likely to be pretty good - especially if you have a partner who you want to please.

It isn't easy for you to find someone worthy of your interest, but once you're sure it is not easy to rebuff you. Timidity soon changes to tenacity and you won't accept no as an answer. Once you have decided to set up a home, you will put all your energies into ensuring that home life is as close to perfect as it can possibly get.

However close your relationship, you need to keep a few secrets - and possibly also a little money hidden away. A deep sense of loyalty coupled with possessiveness means that you try to hold onto a relationship for as long as possible. If the worst happens and the marriage fails, it is hard for you to deal with feelings of rejection.

Your chief faults are moodiness, possessiveness and cruelty. You can give a partner the silent treatment for weeks on end and your sarcastic remarks can drive your partner away. You must guard against being so wrapped up in your own feelings that you forget that you lover has a few of his or her own.

With a Fire Sign Partner

This starts off well, but after the first flush of emotional and physical love, the way that you perceive the relationship working will differ. When this partnership works well, it buzzes with excitement and feeling.

Cancer/Aries

This can be a volatile combination. You like the idea of being with someone who takes the initiative and you appreciate the differences between you, but Aries can become bored with your sensitivity. If you have good lines of communication between you and mutual respect, this might work.

Cancer/Leo

You are ready to offer Leo plenty of admiration, and in return Leo offers complete loyalty. This has great possibilities, but you mustn't keep too tight a hold on the purse strings, because Leo won't suffer unnecessary poverty.

Cancer/Sagittarius

Your desire for security and the Sagittarian need for freedom don't blend. You can't stand Sagittarius's tactless and your sideways manner of going about things can infuriate the Sagittarian.

With an Earth Sign Partner

This is a fairly good mix, as you both need security in a relationship, but you need to find a way of talking to each other rather than hiding your feelings.

Cancer/Taurus

This can be a nurturing and comfortable relationship for both of you so this has the potential to be long lasting. Don't allow miserliness to become a shared way of life - there are other things that you can do rather than merely concentrating on building a huge bank balance.

Cancer/Virgo

Your desire for security can be a bit much for Virgo, especially as the Virgoan doesn't need to be reminded of his obligations, but your outlook is similar and there are many shared attitudes, so this relationship has possibilities.

Cancer/Capricorn

You understand each other's needs and you are happy to fulfil them, but there is little excitement and the partnership could become boring. Sex can fizzle out.

With an Air Sign Partner

This is a difficult combination because you need to give an air sign partner plenty of space and this is not something that comes easily to you. The air sign partner will want to be off doing things while you prefer to stay quietly at home.

Cancer/Gemini

The Gemini habit of flitting about will upset you. Gemini's tendency to nag, worry and moan can make you depressed.

Cancer/Libra

You may make Libra feel crowded and this could be a difficult combination, but you both need partners on whom you can rely, so it might work.

Cancer/Aquarius

Your tendency to cling will drive Aquarius away, also Aquarius can be too selfish for your liking. A very stressful combination.

With A Water Sign Partner

This is a strong combination that works well together because you share similar emotional traits and you offer each other security. You have a strong psychic bond and you both tune into the situations that are around you. If you both become depressed at the same time you will both fall into a sea of despair.

Cancer/Cancer

There's certainly enough understanding between you to make this work. You won't need anyone else, as your own little world will be enough for both of you.

Cancer/Scorpio

A good match because you both need loyalty and devotion, so you are able to supply one another with the security you both need.

Cancer/Pisces

Deep emotional contact can be made and the two of you should feel comfortable together, although you may be irritated by Pisces' unreliability.

Starting a Family

You are a born parent, and in some ways you may almost be too good because you become upset when your children try to assert their independence. You will provide a good home and nothing will be too much trouble for you. You tend to look back to the past for guidance, so your approach to childcare is likely to be very traditional - and you will have no scruples about asking your mother's advice.

For the Cancer woman being pregnant is like a dream come true and once you have achieved this you will want to do it again. Pregnancy offers you the perfect excuse to indulge yourself in baking bread, making little outfits and discovering all those skills a mother is supposed to have. Little else matters in your life apart from your baby. The antique crib is highly polished and your home will be organized so that baby can take pride of place. You might have to make an effort to remember that dad has a role in all this as well. There will be no new birthing ideas for you, because the tried and true is best and you will be happy to listen to mother.

With a Fire Sign Child

Be careful not to overindulge your child because he will learn to take advantage of you, although an occasional treat is a good idea. This child can infuriate you by being rash and this can lead to arguments and displays of temperament on both sides.

With an Earth Sign Child

This child needs security so this works well. However, you will need to take account of their obstinate nature because it can be very difficult for him to change his mind. You will need to encourage him to be more flexible.

With an Air Sign Child

Guard against crowding this child or you could end up losing him. He needs space and freedom far more than constant attention. This child needs fresh air and outward-bound excursions and you will need to encourage him rather than simply to mother him.

With a Water Sign Child

A very good match - particularly for mothers and daughters. You and your child will have a strong psychic link. This child enjoys being mollycoddled and ultimately this is something you will both need to control. You will share each other's secrets but you will also need to ensure that your child grow up to be independent.

Adult Relationships

This next section talks about relationships with parents and parental figures once you yourself are an adult.

With a Fire Sign Parent

This parent will motivate you but he may sometimes become angry and frustrated with you due to your need to take things slowly and in your own stride. Your parent will think he is helping you - perhaps even propping you up, but you may feel that he is trying to pressurize you into behaving in a certain way.

With an Earth Sign Parent

This is generally a good blend, because an earth sign parent offers stability and help. This parent will try to carry out your wishes and he will want to be part of your family.

With an Air Sign Parent

This can be difficult from your point of view, as your parents will tend to leave you alone and not want to be involved in your life. Although good for mutual interests, your parents can sometimes appear to be a little distant and cold.

With a Water Sign Parent

Although the bond is emotionally firm, you must try to separate from each other, particularly if the marriage partner doesn't also belong to a water sign. This relationship can be so close that there is a danger of cutting your partner out.

In-laws and Similar Relationships

Family is everything to you, but you are cautious about whom you love and whom you trust. You will be superficially polite and friendly while allowing your instincts and psychic insight to assess your in-laws before committing yourself fully. Once you decide that they are decent people, you include them fully into your heart, mind and life. However, if you decide that they are not worthy of your trust, you keep them at arm's length and you can actually be quite nasty to them.

Although we are not really dealing with sons or daughters-in-law in this book, I must mention that your tendency towards defensiveness can make you an extremely unpleasant in-law. If you truly dislike your child's spouse, either hide your feelings or keep out of their way. If you must see your own child on a regular basis, do so without his or her partner being present.

With Fire Sign In-laws

This is quite a good match, as long as the in-laws don't interfere with your life. However, if they take it into their heads to take charge of your developing family, your instinct will be to push them away. This could lead to a long-term problem by pitching your family against your partner's family. With mutual respect and a less hands-on approach by all concerned, this can work well.

With Earth Sign In-laws

This is a good match as you can share the same ideals. They will always be willing to offer advice and help, so you should be willing to take it. You may find Virgo in-laws a little critical and possibly a little too clever for your liking, but you still understand their need to help. Earth sign people like to talk and you like to listen, so this works quite well.

With Air Sign In-laws

This can be a difficult relationship. You see them as part of your family, whereas they prefer to lead their own lives and they can find your habit of joining in a bit restrictive. You need to let them know that you're there when they want you, but you should avoid hang around so much that you bore them. They won't want to interfere in your life and they should approve of the way you are bringing up the family and your attitude to their son or daughter. They will probably think of you as dull but stable.

With Water Sign In-laws

A strong match that will work well. You may even share family holidays or live together as one huge extended family at times, but you should guard against involving yourself too much in each other's lives.

Grandchildren

There will be a wonderful relationship between you and your grandchildren, and you will especially enjoy being left in charge of them so that you can feed them treats and spoil them shamelessly. Best of all, you are less likely simply to spend money on your grandchildren than to sit and read to them, help them to draw pictures and play gently. You will even help them with their sports, games and their homework.

With Siblings
You quite like taking the role of pseudo-parent to your siblings. Depending upon the nature and age of the siblings, they will either welcome this or see you as a domineering bossy-boots who tries to interfere.

Choosing a Pet
Some Cancerians love animals, others can't be bothered with them. If you do buy a pet, it will probably be a cat.

Your Vehicle
Believe it or not, your sign is second in line for making insurance claims (after Aries), so you need a safe car. Once you find something that you like, you keep to the same make. You give the car a name and consider it to be part of the family, so you won't be in a hurry to change it in for a new one.

Leo

24 July to 23 August
Gender: Masculine
Element: Fire
Quality: Fixed
Planet: The Sun
Symbol: The Lion

Your Character

Your sign suggests that you are the traditional leader of the Zodiac, as Leo is the sign of kingship. As with all fire signs, you believe in your own ability and you try to maintain a positive attitude even when life goes against you. Your sign symbolizes pride, authority and rulership and many political and world leaders have this sign as a major constituent of their birth charts - if not as a sun sign, then frequently as a rising sign.

Needless to say, you enjoy taking charge of situations and you also crave recognition. You don't play second fiddle to anyone, so are often at the top of a project or enterprise, organizing it brilliantly and making it run smoothly. Despite the fact that this is the traditional view, I have noticed from the many readings I have given to clients over the years that this aspect of your character sometimes takes time to emerge. You sometimes need to be pushed or volunteered into this position, because you can be reticent when outside your home environment. You care about other people and you are very good at encouraging others to take control of situations or to take responsibility. Some of you prefer to be the power behind the scenes than to stand in the limelight yourself. Your zodiac sign represents the father, so it demonstrates all the aspects that you would expect from a father or grandfather figure. You can offer sound advice and take control of situations, and you have the virtue of being able to understand when there is a need for discipline, control and leadership. You can occasionally be a little overbearing and too strict but even this usually comes from a basis of compassion and caring. You can lose your temper when you are fatigued. I know all about this one because my Leo sister often loses her temper when she is tired! Sometimes this display of temper is a way of letting off steam or a form of dramatics.

You can earn very good money from almost any line of work, although you will often make a career choice work for you in a roundabout way rather than by taking the obvious route. You have a knack for being in the right place at the right time, which allows you to take full advantage of a situation. Despite your talent for earning money, your preference for a comfortable, glamorous and pleasurable lifestyle means that you tend to spend more than you can afford. You also spend a fortune on your loved ones - either because you love them or to get them off your back - and this can drain your finances in no time at all.

Although you work hard, you know how to relax and this has the strange effect of setting you up for accusations of laziness. If you picture a pride of lions lying about under a tree for a day or so after they have had eaten - they aren't lazy, it is just that their work has been done. You are intensely proud, so like any lion or lioness, you take immense pride in your children and you love having them around. Being hot on discipline, you need to guard against being a bit too bossy at times.

At work, you won't put up with anything that you dislike and you don't enjoy being used by others. You are an extremely loyal employee providing that you feel that you are being treated fairly; when you are not appreciated or well treated, you find another job as soon as possible. You enjoy your work but you can make mistakes due to acting too quickly or having somewhat unrealistic expectations.

You may turn your love of drama to your advantage by working in the entertainment fields of acting and films, while being keen to protect other people, you can also drift into work as an insurance or estate agent. Other careers that attract your sign are the travel industry, the hotel industry, health and racquet clubs and marketing. You can make a living in any trade that is devoted to leisure and pleasure or that has an aura glamour and prestige. Your drawback is a tendency towards arrogance and bossiness, which can cause problems with colleagues. Another drawback is your habit of expressing honest opinions when a bit of tact might serve you better.

Like fatigue, hunger is another trigger for irritability and bad moods. Your blood sugar tends to fall quickly, so you can feel extremely out of sorts or when hungry. Worse still hunger affects your concentration and gives you strange feelings of being out of control and unable to cope. You should always keep a supply of raisins handy for those occasions when you have to go without food for a while.

The Leo Child

The Leo child wants to be the best and he craves the approval and admiration of his family and his peers. If he doesn't receive this or if others ridicule him, he can become extremely despondent. Leo children like to be the top in their field, but if that is not possible they will settle for being popular. They enjoy getting involved with groups and they soon show themselves as leader and spokesman. At home, this child soon learns how to get his own way and he can play on his parents' feelings.

These children are bright and they have an instinct for performing, so such things as training in dancing, acting and music are always welcome to them. This youngster likes to dress well and look good, but if he is at home with nothing special to do, he won't bother with his appearance. It is as though he is either totally on show, or happy simply to relax and slob out.

Sex and the Single Leo

You set your lover on a pedestal, but you want the admiration to be mutual, because you also need to be admired, but you are also capable of great loyalty. Knowing that one person is devoted to you gives you a special glow. Astrology books tell us that you are likely to be very fond of yourself and that flattery will always please you. This is true for some Leos, but many are too intelligent to be taken in by blatant flattery. A partner who acts as a servant and who doesn't have a mind of his or her own is a nice idea, but this scenario would soon bore you rigid. Indeed, you prefer one of whom you can be proud.

Sometimes your expectations are unrealistic - for instance, you tend to be possessive but you hate to feel possessed. On balance you are loyal and generous and you can be an incredibly devoted lover and you can take on the role of protector. Love is a matter of impulse and you imbue it with a sense of drama that other signs can only dream of. More than anything you seek admiration, so Leo men can be lady-killers and Leo women seek admiration from whoever will bestow it, but you are also an extravagant and ostentatious lover. All told, you are powerful and sincere, wholehearted and generous.

When it comes to sex you're proud of your agility and expertise - so proud that you might actually enjoy being surrounded by mirrors in these circumstances, and you may exaggerate your abilities. This enjoyment of display means that you're one of the few signs that may be drawn to lap dancing and strip shows.

The world will always know when you have someone special in sight, and this isn't superficial, because your feelings are sincere and you have no problem in showing them. One of your worst faults is that you soon become bored with a lover, so you need to choose someone who has the capacity to fascinate you over a very long period of time.

Marriage and Partnership

The passion you express can be exciting in the first throes of romance but jealousy can follow and that can cause a problem in the long term. The fact is that you need your partner to belong to you heart and soul, and remaining faithful isn't a problem for you. You certainly enjoy an active social life and you are a natural flirt, but you won't waste time chasing after others if there is someone special in your life. Although your eyes may wander from time to time that's usually as far as it goes.

Your love of luxury and capacity for generosity is great fun in the early days of a romance, but when it comes to settling down this extravagance can cause problems. You like things to look good and want to feel superior to those around you, so you may become attracted to a person who makes you look good by association. Down-market people and losers need not apply for even a short-lived relationship with you - let alone marriage. You need a partner who you can respect.

With a Fire Sign Partner

Although plenty of excitement is on offer, you both want to come first and the fire energy that you share can be a bit hot to handle at times, so you might end up fighting one another. You have plenty in common, including boundless energy; but some compromise will be essential in order to avoid this being merely a short-lived romance.

Leo/Aries

This is an explosive combination with a lot of potential for clashes. Unless one of you can learn to compromise regularly, this will be a short, although exciting, romance.

Leo/Leo

This is either incredibly wonderful or an utter disaster, depending on whether one of you is capable of relinquishing some control.

Leo/Sagittarius

Superficially you get on well, but Sagittarius isn't as constant as you would like, while you may be too demanding for Sagittarius, although you may have enough in common to make this combination work.

With an Earth Sign Partner

It can be hard for your partner to keep up with you; you live life at different speeds, and your partner's slower pace may frustrate you at times. You may also feel that your partner is holding you back, although he or she may simply be trying to keep you away from your worst excesses. Earth sign people can be very obstinate which can infuriate you. You will generate the excitement you need in a relationship, while the partner is left to take charge of the practicalities.

Leo/Taurus

The Taurean will not appreciate your desire to take control and he may not be prepared or able to offer you the attention that you seek. This is not an obvious success.

Leo/Virgo

This depends somewhat on the kind of Virgo that you find yourself dealing with. If it is the fussy, neurotic type of person who holds back from life, you will soon find yourself becoming bored and frustrated. If the Virgo partner has a quick mind and deep intellect, coupled with a sense of humor and no fusspot ideas, this can work well. The sex might be good too.

Leo/Capricorn

This can be a very physical combination but there could be difficulties in other areas. Capricorn is even more ambitious than you are which means that you could both want to take center stage. Capricorn resents your spending habits.

With an Air Sign Partner

Air and fire makes a volatile mixture but it can work well in a love relationship, because air sign people offer encouragement and enthusiasm. One problem is that air signs like to think things through before embarking on them while you prefer acting on impulse. If you want the relationship to last you will need to work at it.

Leo/Gemini

Gemini soon learns to manipulate you, and Gemini may not be the constant and loyal companion you need. Worse still, Gemini can be self-absorbed and inclined to fuss and worry about small matters - and this will irritate you.

Leo/Libra

You both love luxury and a comfortable lifestyle but it will be up to you to provide the means to obtain this. Your generosity will appeal to Libra's sense of romance but you are unlikely to treat Libra with the gentleness he wants. Librans can switch off or even pick a fight once they have finished making love and that won't suit you at all.

Leo/Aquarius

There is so much variation within Aquarius that it could work if the right one comes along. Most Aquarians have many fish to fry, so they are unlikely to pay you the attention that you need, but on the other hand they won't try to crowd you.

With a Water Sign Partner

This can work well in a traditional partnership where Leo is the breadwinner and the water sign the homemaker, but as that rarely occurs nowadays this can be a relationship fraught with problems. You will need to provide both financial and emotional security for the pair of you. Your partner's moods and fits of depression or vulnerability will irritate you, and if the partner is confrontational and sarcastic (as some water sign people are), you will become so hurt and despondent that you eventually decide to save your own sanity by leaving them.

Leo/Cancer

Cancer is ready to offer plenty of admiration and in return you can offer Cancer complete loyalty. This has great possibilities.

Leo/Scorpio

Both of you are stubborn. This is only possible if you are willing to accept one another as equals. You are unlikely to offer the respect that Scorpio desires.

Leo/Pisces

It is difficult to combine your morals and values with Pisces unreliability. Also, you are highly organized while Pisces prefers a fluid and chaotic lifestyle.

Starting a Family

As a Leo woman you're unlikely to worry about pregnancy, and it's obvious that your child is bound to be perfect. As enthusiastic about pregnancy as you are about everything else in life, you soon start to express your opinions about how things should go. Anyone listening to you would think that you're the first woman to go through this, so your childless friends will find their eyes glazing over while you give them all the latest details. You're happy enough to join any prenatal group going - and within no time at all you'll probably run it. As soon as the moment of birth arrives and you become the center of attention, you relax and enjoy it, because that is exactly where you want to be. Your children will soon become the most important part of your life and you

will do all you can and make every possible sacrifice in order
to make them happy.

With a Fire Sign Child

This is a strong combination because you will give your
child the encouragement he needs. It is great when you pull
together, otherwise there can be tension, but this child will
give you the affection that you crave.

With an Earth Sign Child

As long as your child shows an interest in something,
you will encourage it. He may only start to make an effort
once he leaves childhood behind and you may feel frustrated
by this.

With an Air Sign Child

You will share your child's enthusiasms but you might
become irritated by his lack of concentration. If you can work
together on projects - and if you can take overall charge - this
is fine. Problems may come when the child wants to detach
from you, wander off and follow his own star - which may be
a very different one from that which you had in mind.

With a Water Sign Child

Your child's moodiness and slowness may confuse and
irritate you but you will offer the depth of love and reassurance
that this child needs.

Adult Relationships

Relationships with your parents and others will be fine
as long as they understand that you are an adult and that you
should be treated as such.

With a Fire Sign Parent

When it works well this is a strong combination as you can both move in the same direction and share the same ideals, but if you disagree there can be problems, perhaps in many ways because you are too alike. This is a relationship that often has to be worked at.

With an Earth Sign Parent

This is generally a good combination because earth sign parents can offer practical help and understanding but you cannot operate in the same practical and sustained manner that they do. No matter how much they disapprove of the things that you do with your life, they will always be there for you.

With an Air Sign Parent

Your parents will support your decisions even when they don't agree with them. At times you'll wish they could offer more practical help and their detached and independent manner will make you feel that they are not interested in helping you.

With a Water Sign Parent

This is not the best blend, because this parent's tendency to become emotional or take offence over nothing may spoil the relationship. The parent will be there to give you the support you need help, although you may see this as interference. You will also hate this parent's habit of talking about the past.

In-laws and Similar Relationships

You are happy to work at these relationships with these folk, as long as they don't criticize you or interfere.

With Fire Sign In-laws

Although you may share many of the same interests this isn't always a very good combination. You both want to be the center of your partner's universe, so this could lead to feelings of jealousy. Differences of opinion are likely to lead to major explosions, so you may need to bite your tongue once in a while.

With Earth Sign In-laws

They want to be helpful while you want to do things your way. There are times when you might be grateful for their help, so it would be best not to reject them out of hand. If you run into any financial problems, it's good to know that you have someone to call on. They may be unnerved by your exuberance and impetuousness and they might envy you, but they have abilities you don't, so it could balance out.

With Air Sign In-laws

You both enjoy social interaction so this can be pleasant as long as the relationship remains fairly superficial. You may need to remind yourself that the bright ideas that they come up with really are bright. You are very different from them, but with care you can complement each other.

With Water Sign In-laws

This is not an easy situation, as you will find yourself offending your in-laws without knowing what it is that you have said. They may cling to your partner and interfere in your life, but they can be useful - even if only for their services as baby-sitters.

Grandchildren
There is no question that you will spoil and indulge your grandchildren, but you won't tolerate rudeness, greed or bad behavior. If your grandchildren are reasonable, you will be too.

With Siblings
You are a wonderful brother or sister, as long as you can be the boss! You may resent the share of attention that your siblings receive from your parents, but you soon find other places where you can be in the center of things.

Choosing a Pet
You love beautiful animals, such as pedigree cats and good horses. If you decide on a dog, you may end up with something larger than you can handle. You actually enjoy very small animals like hamsters and attractive fish.

Your Vehicle
Being a sunny fire sign, you may prefer a red or yellow car. You are keen to protect your children, so you look for safety features such as child locks and a good braking system.

Virgo

24 August - 23 September
Gender: Feminine
Element: Earth
Quality: Mutable
Planet: Mercury
Symbol: The Maiden

Your Character

Virgo is symbolized by the corn maiden who represents the fruits of labor and the harvest that is yet to come, so it's not too surprising that you belong to one of the most hard-working signs of the zodiac.

Your analytical mind and Mercurial intelligence take you far, and indeed many captains of industry belong to your sign. Being highly organized and extremely capable, it is unlikely that you will spend your life sitting about watching daytime television or allowing yourself to drift. If there is a job to be done, either at home or out in the wider world, you get on with it. You are far too talkative and friendly to be a silent mouse, so your life is filled with friends, activities, interests and trips hither and thither as you rush around to fit twenty five hours' worth of living into each day.

Being an earth sign, you are practical and very good at paying attention to detail. Indeed, many of you work as editors, where your ability to spot an error while checking through a text at the speed of light comes to your aid. Your sign is ruled by Mercury, the messenger of the gods, so you love nothing more than talking on the phone for business purposes and also spending time chatting with friends and running up your telephone bill. Your keen skills of observation give you the ability to understand others, to look deeply into things and to analyze people and systems, and this means that you can succeed as a psychologist or business analyst. Despite this acumen, you are often more successful analyzing others than you are in knowing yourself.

You value loyalty very highly and you are amazingly reliable and dependable - and in a world of people who fade away when trouble advances, you constitute a real rock that your friends can lean on. You have more than the usual amount of love and attention to spend on other people, and it is not unusual for you to sacrifice yourself for the aid of someone else. It is not surprising then that many of you are attracted to careers in medicine, the care of animals and social work. You are so generous with your time that you need to take care that you don't give so much or work so hard that you become overstressed.

Many of you born are quite reticent which means that you may not appear particularly affectionate. You can only bear to be touched and hugged by those who are extremely close to you, but the fact is that this could cause problems in relationships because your lovers may think you don't feel very much for them. You prefer to show your love by cooking a nice meal, taking care of your partner and by making love.

The chances are that your parents or schoolteachers made you feel insignificant and ashamed for no real purpose.

As an adult, you are a true approval-seeker, and you want to be seen as hard working, generous, caring, decent and worthwhile, so their sarcastic comments were damaging and completely unnecessary. You may have incurred the wrath of these adults by your habit of talking at the wrong time or by asking too many questions. Not everybody has all that much use for such an intelligent child. Naturally, this has left a legacy of insecurity and low self-esteem means that you hesitate to put your trust into others, and another result of this is that in adult life you become an extreme perfectionist. This is valuable when you are doing work where perfection is important but you may be irritatingly pernickety. Sometimes this is a way of preventing life from spinning out of control and into a form of unimaginable chaos.

You are too quick to criticize others and this can lead to problems in relationships because there will come a time when the other person begins to feel that they can't do anything right. Remember to lighten up and to praise people as well as point out their faults and failings. You set extremely high standards for yourself and you can become stressed and self-critical if you fail to live up to your own expectations.

Astrology books always harp on about your tidiness, but while some of you live in tidy homes and are always neat and well groomed, others are the complete opposite. However, you usually know where everything is and you hate other people to touch your things or to tidy them up. On the face of things it seems surprising that for such a down to earth sign, many of you are interested in astrology. Actually this is not so surprising because, people fascinate you and so do analytical systems - and astrology combines both these factors. Your desire to help people - indeed to rescue them from pain can lead you into a life as a consultant in this field.

In your worst moments, you might retreat into hypochondria and fussiness, perhaps also insisting that your partner and children maintain standards of achievement or housekeeping that are beyond reason.

The Virgo Child

Generally this child is quite tidy, and even if this is not the case you will discover that this child is mentally tidy and also logical. He will enjoy solving puzzles and he can store a great deal of information in his mind. Looking at my son, Daniel, who at the time of writing this is twelve years of age - he may be extremely untidy but the filing system in his mind contains the names of every Manchester United soccer player and every one of their previous football clubs

This child is likely to suffer from a lack of self-confidence, which means that he will need reassurance from you in order to build his self-esteem. He may be a late developer. Being an earth sign it is very difficult to push him when he doesn't want to do something or doesn't want to learn. He can become belligerent and obstinate, but if he becomes committed to a course of action that he believes in, he will persevere. He will eventually seek out a career in which he gives service to others, possibly as a professional in the health arena, the catering industry, teaching or some form of research.

Sex and the Single Virgo

Just because Virgo is the sign of the Maiden or Virgin, this does not mean that you are not destined to have a sex life - it is just that you tend to make the bed afterwards! Indeed, yours is a sensual earth sign, so sex is probably more important for your mental and physical health than it is for many other signs.

Your lack of self-worth can cause you to feel that nothing you do is good enough and that you don't deserve love. Flattery doesn't impress you so genuine reassurance and acceptance is important to you in any relationship. Unfortunately, you don't always give the same to those who attach themselves to you, so you may severely test your lovers in order to see how much they will put up with.

You do your best to satisfy your lover but you are not keen on surprises where sex is concerned and you desire stability rather than short-term flings. When you finally find it, you can be incredibly giving and generous but if a lover doesn't live up to your high standards you can easily adapt to life alone. You may have weird fantasies but you are probably too shy to act them out. Many of you eschew sexy underwear in favor of large comfortable, plain white underpinnings. Having said this, you can get into sadomasochism and one Virgo who I know told me that he liked tied up while someone attacked him with a cattle prod! This may sound crazy but it actually makes sense because there is a level at which you feel that you deserve to be punished, possibly because you became accustomed to being mistreated in childhood. Hygiene is important to you and you're the sign most likely to practice safe sex.

Marriage and Partnership
You like to express your affection unselfishly and pragmatically. It may take you a long time to choose the person that you want to spend your life with, but once that choice is made they'll have no doubts about your love. In the early years, you will be more than able to deal with any hardships. If the two of you don't share the home of your dreams you can be sure that it isn't because you haven't made enough effort.

You need to take care and time when choosing a partners. Listen to the advice of your head (and your friends) as well as your heart. If you rush into things, you could find yourself with someone who abuses you, taking everything that they can grab of a mental, emotional and financial nature, while giving very little back. Although you're not the jealous type, you're capable of being highly possessive. Your loyalty means that you hate to destroy family ties, but if you feel that you must leave your partner, then you favor a quick clean break.

With a Fire Sign Partner

It can be hard for you to keep up with your partner - you seem to live life at different speeds. The positive side of this is that you're able to offer stability and consistency to your fire partner's life. If you can encourage your lover to slow down occasionally, you can save him from his own worst excesses. Generally, however, this combination is not ideal.

Virgo/Aries

Spontaneous Aries will consider you to be too critical and you don't like being rushed into things, so this is a difficult combination.

Virgo/Leo

Leo can find you frustrating and too restrained. Having said this, when two signs are adjacent, the chances are that you have planets in each other's signs and that can lead to surprising amount of compatibility.

Virgo/Sagittarius

With Sagittarius focusing on adventure and you on commitment, this makes for an unlikely love match, although there is plenty of scope for friendship based on mutual interests in academic or spiritual subjects.

With an Earth Sign Partner

This is an excellent combination because you think alike and you are both are very stable. You can work well together but you can both be stubborn, so compromise is an area that you will need to work on. Also you could both get stuck in a rut and forgetting to have fun.

Virgo/Taurus

The two of you can develop warmth between you and confidence in one another. You could well have a sensual and long-term relationship.

Virgo/Virgo

It can work, so long as you don't nag one another into submission.

Virgo/Capricorn

You are both demanding and fussy and your sensitivity means that you can both take offence at the same time. Both can be penny-pinching, so buying bargains might become a mutual interest. There are enough similarities to make this work.

With an Air Sign Partner

This is not a particularly good combination as you find it hard to cope with your air friend's fickleness and butterfly mind. It can take a while for you learn to understand each another but you are both great communicators, so you should get there in the end.

Virgo/Gemini

Gemini is quick to rush into new experiences, while you need security and a long-term relationship. After the initial magnetic attraction, you may decide to wave goodbye to Gemini.

Virgo/Libra

Libra may be put off by your boldness, but this combination will work if you allow time to get to know each other.

Virgo/Aquarius

A long-term relationship is unlikely as Aquarius finds it hard to comply with your need for practicality and an organized lifestyle.

With a Water Sign Partner

You both need security in a relationship so this could be a good combination, but to make it really work you will need to find a way to communicate, rather than hiding your feelings. You might get frustrated with a water sign person's sensitivity and emotionalism, but a little understanding can go a long way.

Virgo/Cancer

Cancer's desire for security can be a bit much for you because you don't need reminding of your obligations. You share similar attitudes towards many things so this relationship has possibilities.

Virgo/Scorpio

This is a highly dynamic combination as the two signs have much to offer one another. You are both perfectionists in your way and the shared level of intelligence means that you can chat easily to each other.

Virgo/ Pisces
This combination can be ideal, as your earthiness combines well with the Piscean depth and sensitivity, but you could resent your lover's unreliability.

Starting a Family
Keeping your newborn baby clean and healthy is a priority, and in the early days, you may well focus on this aspect of life more than any other. You will find it hard to relax as there's always something that needs to be done, so there will be times when you need to remind yourself to stop rushing around and simply to sit and enjoy your child's company. Your baby won't mind if your home is not in pristine condition.

As a Virgo woman, you can organize your pregnancy extremely well. Not only will you have the nursery ready and the baby's name chosen, but will probably put its name put down for a good school as well. Health matters to you, so you will plan for the least possible medical intervention. However, you will need to keep sight of the fact that a new person is about to arrive in your life - and pregnancy and labor have a habit of throwing the best timetables out of the window, so you need to be flexible.

With a Fire Sign Child
This child's rebellious attitude will sometimes be difficult to deal with, but his sense of adventure and desire to experiment with clothes, music and different interests will fascinate you. You need to make an effort to see things from this child's point of view and also encourage him to finish

what he starts. Give him the stability and validation that he needs and he will make you very proud of his achievements.

With an Earth Sign Child

Take care not to criticize this child too much as cutting remarks will damage him. Disagreements will cause clashes due to your child's strong will, and you will have to find a means of meeting each other half way. Your child will happily cope with schoolwork, and details won't throw him, but don't expect him to do things quickly.

With an Air Sign Child

This may be a difficult combination, because you are systematic and this child will flit from one idea to another and change his plans at the drop of a hat. You can give him the security that he needs but you also need to give him freedom. Lay off the criticism as much as possible.

With a Water Sign Child

This can be a difficult combination as you will find this child's emotionalism hard to handle and you may also find it hard to get him to focus and concentrate on things of an academic nature. You can offer this child plenty of support and encouragement, although it may take time to sort out difficult areas of life, you usually manage to do so in the end.

Adult Relationships

This next section talks about your relationships as an adult with parents and parental figures.

With a Fire Sign Parent

This is not a particularly good combination as there could be a clash of wills. Your stubbornness and practicality can get in the way of this parent's enthusiasm and you may feel that you are not necessarily meeting the standards he sets.

With an Earth Sign Parent

This is potentially a good match as you share the same basic personality and probably the same need for security. However if you do disagree then you could both become stubborn, making it hard to find a solution. This is a combination when it works well but when it doesn't it is painful.

With an Air Sign Parent

As far parental relationships go, the only problem is that you may occasionally wish they were more forthcoming with practical help. They are enthusiastic about your ideas and they will happily offer suggestions, but you may want them to get a bit more involved than they are prepared to do.

With a Water Sign Parent

Potentially this is a good mixture as there should be strong emotional bonds between you and it this likely to be a very supportive relationship, but they can be very emotional and you could find this a bit cloying. Your stubborn moods could cause problems.

In-laws and Similar Relationships

This section deals with your relationships with adults who are attached to you but are not blood relatives.

With Fire Sign In-laws

This can be difficult because these people may not appreciate your efforts to help them, and you may resent having to bail them out of their latest disaster. You won't persuade them to think things through before acting, so it isn't worth wasting your energy trying, but they will certainly bring some excitement into your life.

With Earth Sign In-laws

No real problems here, as you get along so well that you find it easy to slot into their lives, and you may even find yourself being taken into the family business. Certainly, they can be very helpful to you in your career plans.

With Air Sign In-laws

You don't really get on, as you tend to find these people a little superficial. If you're working together to achieve something you can produce results, but your shared tendency to ignore feelings can cause problems.

With Water Sign In-laws

You get on quite happily with these, much of the time, but they may want more closeness than you need. You may consider their helpfulness to be interference.

Grandchildren

If you are a grandparent, you will thoroughly enjoy taking your grandchildren out and introducing them to the world of books and ideas. You will share their interest in children's television programs and you will happily spend money on their clothes and interests.

With Siblings

If your sisters and brothers are sociable, pleasant and cooperative, you will be too - otherwise you will simply keep out of their way. You have plenty of friends, so you don't need contact with brothers and sisters - but you will want this anyway if the relationships are pleasant.

Choosing a Pet

You prefer small breeds of dogs, small caged animals and tropical fish. Cats suit you because they are clean, graceful and independent.

Your Vehicle

You belong to the ranks of safe and cautious drivers and you don't like taking risks, so insurance companies report that you have relatively few accidents. You are the least likely of all the zodiac signs to buy a new car, but you still want your car to look new, clean and untouched and you prefer the color white.

Libra

24 September to 23 October
Gender: Masculine
Element: Air
Quality: Cardinal
Planet: Venus
Symbol: The Scales

Your Character

Venus is a planet that inclines you to be somewhat slow to take action and to be lazy and self-indulgent at times. You can potter about with those things that interest you at one time, and put all that cardinal, masculine verve into doing active things at another. All of this means that you can switch between lazing on the sofa and stretching like a cat between snoozes, and then spinning around like a Dervish and getting everything done in the wink of an eye. We all tend to think of Venus as the planet of love - and so it is: but it is also the planet of sex, and also, believe it or not, of fighting and of war. Libra and Venus are both associated with partnerships and relationships with others, so these will always be important, both in terms of your personal life and business or work. However, these factors are also associated with open enemies, so you are as likely to have to put up a fight at times during your life, as you are to snuggle down with your partner for a bit of truly Venusian love-making. Added to this is the detachment and need for space and freedom that being an air sign endows.

Librans have a reputation for indecisiveness, although in my opinion, you can make decisions quite easily, as long as you are not rushed into them. It is not surprising that any decision is hard for you to come by, as you have all these conflicting and confusing factors within your character to cope with. Your sign of the scales indicates that you like to balance and weigh things up in your mind before going ahead with anything. Sometimes you can miss the boat because you spend too much time weighing things up and asking the opinions of those who are around you. Sometimes you listen to the advice that others give you, and then do the exact opposite - often to your own detriment. Also, if someone tries to rush you or commit you to a deadline, a weird kind of obstinacy kicks in and you can simply put the job aside and do something that is less important while making the other person wait for whatever it is that they want. The more people pressurize you, the slower and less interested you become.

You want to enjoy life to the full, and your charming and easygoing nature allows you to get on with most people. Being a born diplomat, you will try to find a way of getting what you want by reasoned logic rather than by fighting, but if you have to fight, there is nobody better able to do so. Your desire for justice means that you will often step in on the side of an underdog.

Everything that you consider is a form of comparison, because you need to understand the pros and cons of any issue, and then try to make a measured judgement. Being an air sign, you are not short of ideas, you are happy to give others the benefit of your wisdom and to advise them on how to run their lives. You find it easier to sort out the problems of others than your own problems and so you can succeed at working on behalf of others and thus find yourself working as a lawyer, judge, policeman or counselor of some kind.

You love a good old gossip and you thoroughly enjoy being in the know, so you spend hours chatting to friends and colleagues. The same goes for keeping abreast of trends, which means that you know the latest hit record, the state of the nation's budget and what is going on in your neighborhood. Some Librans drone on as if they are addressing an audience, and they may be far fonder of the sound of their own voices than they are of conversing and listening to what others have to say. Others are good listeners and happy to interact in a normal manner.

Being so double sided, you can balance this need for news by an equal need to hide from reality - especially when the reality in question turns out to be a problem that concerns you personally. You can live in a dream world which quickly becomes real to you, despite all the evidence to the contrary.

Despite your laid-back manner, you really can't cope well with stress, and if something serious happens, you may become sick or retreat from life in some way. One Libran man who I knew became paralyzed when under severe work related stress and his poor wife thought that he was suffering from a stroke. After a few days in bed, the paralysis gradually eased and they both took the decision that he should leave the job and find something less well paid but far less stressful.

The Libra Child

Appearance is very important to this child, so he will always want the latest clothes, fashion accessories and toys. The latter doesn't arise out of a real desire for the toy in question but from a need to be the first among his friends to have something and to enjoy showing it to other children and letting others play with it. Indeed, this child may lend his possessions out to other children in order to gain their friendship.

Libran children are musical and artistic, so this should be encouraged. Even if you would prefer your child to look for a safe job, the chances are that he will want to be an actor, artist or musician - and it is a fact that many of the best musicians have been Librans. This child will take up any career where he can be diplomatic and understanding and where he can bring beauty, joy and success to others.

Sex and the Single Libran

Idealistic to a fault, you're more in love with the idea of love than you can actually be with any one person and you may spend your life searching for the perfect partner. Love is important to you, but equally important if that you should remember not to try comparing your current lover with one that you once loved and lost. Your natural charm is a great help in attracting others to your side, but you're not the most obviously sexual of signs. You hate to hurt anyone's feelings, which means that you rarely turn down any offers that are made to you, and this is why some of you can be very promiscuous. You might be unsure of exactly what you're looking for, so the idea of being close to one person alone doesn't really suit you, or perhaps it defeats the object because you need the freedom to keep on searching for the perfect partner. You are perfectly capable of committing yourself to another, deciding that you have got it all wrong and then leaving the poor partner without a word of explanation.

When you do have someone in your life, your behavior towards your lover is gallant and immaculate, and you have the ability to tune into what they want. This is nice, but something that is far less pleasant is the fact that you are more than capable of playing off one admirer against another. You respond to admiration and flattery - even when you're perfectly aware that it is simply flattery. Reality is so unpleasant to you that you often choose to ignore it. You are quite a party animal and you tend to lose your inhibitions quickly when in good company. Being a consummate flirt, you hope for sympathy, love and understanding from everyone you meet, but while you have an affectionate manner you can also be selfish and shallow.

When it comes to sex you're easily bored with routine so you can be extremely accommodating to the desires of your lover, especially if your lover comes up with something that will make a nice change. On the negative side there is a temptation for you to use sex to manipulate and control others or worse still to institute an argument in order to rev up the atmosphere and make sex more exciting.

Marriage and Partnership

You're at your best in the early stages of a relationship. Once your courtship tactics have borne fruit you aren't so sure what the next move should be, and as you hate to refuse or offend anyone, there may be many close calls before the decision to marry is finally made. When you set out to explain why you don't want to marry or make a commitment, your honesty is absolutely pure but the news you dish out is rarely what your partner needs to hear. Once settled, you need an orderly home, and a quiet oasis from all the discord of the outside world. You prefer space and tidiness to clutter and mess and you love to surround yourself with luxury and comfort, and you are prepared to spend whatever it takes to get just that.

With a Fire Sign Partner

Fire sign people are so enthusiastic that they are off down the road doing something at the drop of a hat, while you like to give due consideration to all the possibilities before acting. This can work well if you both appreciate these differences and use the blend of two opposites in a positive way.

Libra/Aries

Aries demands a level of intensity, while you want more commitment and solid romance than Aries may be able to supply. However, this can surprise everyone by turning out to be an enduring and successful relationship where each appreciates the other.

Libra/Leo

Leo is unlikely to treat you gently enough, but his natural generosity and ostentation may appeal to your sense of romance. Leo will also contribute to the kind of wealthy and comfortable lifestyle that you enjoy.

Libra/Sagittarius

This can work if Sagittarius will provide at least a veneer of respectability. Both of you can live in a dream world of your own making though - and as long as these dream worlds coincide, this combination can work.

With an Earth Sign Partner

This can work, because there is a level of sensuality that you both enjoy. Also, you will thoroughly enjoy doing up a home for yourselves, and then inviting plenty of guests along for dinner parties and entertainment. However, the earth partner might be a little too stick-in-the-mud for your liking, while he may find your constant changes hard to cope with.

Libra/Taurus

You both love art, music, gardening, cooking and home making and you both love your family, although you are more detached and less sentimental than your Taurus lover. You are both sensual and quite highly sexed so it could work well. However, the Taurean obstinacy will clash with your determination.

Libra/Virgo

There are enough similarities between you to make this work. You are both highly sexed but neither of you enjoys sloppy displays of affection. Virgo's attention to detail allied to your inventive and artistic mind could ensure a creative partnership.

Libra/Capricorn

Although both of you are conventional in your views, Capricorn may find you a bit too cool and unmotivated. Capricorn's ambition, attention to detail and fussiness may irritate you.

With an Air Sign Partner

This works well, as long as you are both on the same wavelength and as long as you both have enough energy to make things happen and not just to talk about them. This combination often works better for older partners who have developed enough maturity to cope with life.

Libra/Gemini

A cerebral combination that makes communication easy. You share the same kinds of intellectual interests and you both like to be up-to-date and in the know. However, you both could give flirting lessons, so neither of you must be prone to possessiveness or unreasonable jealousy.

Libra/Libra

It is likely that you would be better off as friends than as lovers, as you both love to talk over abstract things and to discuss unrealistic dreams of utopia. However, you are both sexual and sensual, so it may work on a more basic level on a shot-term basis.

Libra/Aquarius

You can both argue the hind leg off a donkey so should both enjoy debating or the relationship may quickly degenerate into fierce and perpetually unresolved arguments. Your aims and drives are similar so it might work if you are prepared to make the effort, but neither one of you is likely to put your whole heart to the relationship.

With a Water Sign Partner

You may find water sign people too emotionally dependent, and their need for constant reassurance might bore you rigid while they will not understand how you can be so cool about emotional issues. Water sign people make decisions and act according to their feelings at any specific moment in time whereas you work from a logical point of view, so you may end up infuriating each other.

Libra/Cancer

The Cancerian may make you feel cramped and swamped, so this could be a difficult combination. Both of you are determined and ambitious, so as long as your ambitions and interests run along the same lines it might just work.

Libra/Scorpio

Both of you can live in a kind of never-never fantasyland, although this takes different forms. Scorpio takes decisions on an almost purely intuitive or psychic level, which will puzzle you. Having said that, where love and passion are concerned the situation is reversed and Scorpio's dream of eternal passionate love doesn't fit with the reality of daily life.

Libra/Pisces

Where you are concerned what you see is pretty much what you get, but with Pisces you wonder what you're looking at. Pisces can be too illogical and too far removed from practicality, even for a dreamer like you.

Starting a Family

The only serious problem for you in starting a new family is that the peace you desire so much in life is inevitably disturbed. You like to have fun with your child right from the start and incorporate the new baby into your social life as soon as you can, so yours is likely to be a lively household where everyone feels welcome. It is best if your partner can take the major decisions for all of you.

As a Libran woman, finding yourself pregnant may take you by surprise because you may not feel quite ready for this - even if the pregnancy is one that is longed for. However excited you are about this new experience, you won't forget to keep the father involved in every stage. There's no way that pregnancy is going to force you into feeling fat and frumpy because it is as important to you to look good while you're pregnant as any other time. You know that if you're going to be at your best, plenty of rest is in order and fortunately you are well able to chill out and relax. You'd prefer the process of birth itself to be a little more decorous than it is, but in the end the sheer pleasure of the new arrival will make it all worthwhile.

With a Fire Sign Child

You want this child to enjoy himself, but you also want him to expand his experiences of life and try different avenues, rather than to focus on one particular interest.

With an Earth Sign Child

Changes in routine will unsettle your child, so you need to aim for a quiet life. His will-power, combined with your tendency to argue the hind leg off a donkey, could lead to major clashes.

With an Air Sign Child

You need to ensure that your son or daughter does not go through life with the same problems you had, so you may need to teach them about some of the pitfalls that you have learned to overcome.

With a Water Sign Child

Your water element child needs reassurance and love and you will have to help him to overcome shyness. You will try to warn him off becoming involved in love relationships to soon.

Adult Relationships
The following section looks at your relationship with parents or parental figures once you are an adult.

With a Fire Sign Parent
A fire sign parent can encourage you to try new things and to develop strength of character. They may become infuriated by your lack of overt ambition and they may have tried to push you when you were young, to no great avail. However, you surprise them later on by doing so much better than expected. Your parent will be there for you whenever you need help and he or she will always be on your side.

With an Earth Sign Parent
There are points of agreement, and others where you clash. Your parent may prefer you to have your feet rather more firmly planted on the ground. Your parent needs a more static life, while you are something of a free spirit and your viewpoints can be very different. This parent will always be on hand when you need financial or practical support. The best combination is Libra and Taurus, because you share the rulership of the planet, Venus, so you may choose similar jobs or have similar interests.

With an Air Sign Parent
This is a strong relationship, but you both lack practicality, so you may end up with a wonderful friendship but neither of you will really be able to rely upon the other when needs must. If you work together, this might be a good relationship because you share the same imaginative flair.

With a Water Sign Parent

He will see himself as offering help, while you will consider this to be interference. Even if you make a mess of your life at some point, you consider this to be your own business. If your parent criticizes you, this will go in one ear and out the other.

In-laws and Similar Relationships

The following section looks at the relationship with in-laws or similar kinds of non-blood links.

With Fire Sign In-laws

You're likely to get along well even if you don't always agree with their attitudes. Also you're both highly sociable so you would all get on well at family parties and the occasional game of golf or a visit to the bowling alley. You enjoy this relative's enthusiasm and energy even thought there are times when you wish they would stop and think things through.

With Earth Sign In-laws

You may find these in-laws a little boring, while they will consider you somewhat superficial, but if you combine together on family projects you can produce results. As long as the earth in-law is sociable, you can enjoy family times together.

With Air Sign In-laws

You share similar interests and you may well enjoy going on adventurous holidays together. You will never be short of something to chat about as you both enjoy a good gossip.

With Water Sign In-laws

This can be a difficult relationship, as they don't want to let you out of their sight. It isn't that they don't trust you; it is simply that they want to be involved as part of your family. This can make you feel restricted at times so it's important to ensure they know that you and your partner have your own lives to lead.

Grandchildren

Looking after grandchildren on a full-time basis would bore you but seeing them on occasion will work well. You love to spoil your grandchildren by buying them the latest gadget or expensive and very up-to-date clothes. If necessary, you will shell out for such things as dentistry and education.

With Siblings

As a child you will fight for your share of parental attention and you will argue with your brothers and sisters. In adulthood you develop a live and let live attitude but you will still disagree with them if you see too much of them. You are better being at a distance as you can then thoroughly enjoy their company on the odd occasion when you get together.

Choosing a Pet

You will only take on an animal that can look after itself or one that looks very good. Therefore, a beautiful Burmese cat is one possibility while tropical fish is another.

Your Vehicle

You love to feel encased in luxury, so the best kind of limo is likely to appeal, and as you also need to squeeze all your friends into your car, it had better be a large one. Your car is part of your image, so you choose a nice, sexy red one.

Scorpio

24 October to 22 November
Gender: Feminine
Element: Water
Quality: Fixed
Planet: Pluto (and Mars)
Symbol: The Scorpion

Your Character

You belong to the most emotional of all the signs, so your feelings and intuition are a major factor in everything that you do. You can even make snap decisions based purely on your feelings, and while your instinct is usually spot on, when you do occasionally make the wrong choice, it is really wrong! Yours is probably the most intense sign of the zodiac, so you cannot live on the surface of life, do a mundane job or live in a mundane marriage.

You have a sharp brain and you are an excellent communicator but you do have that notable sting in your tail. You sometimes speak out bluntly, which can be costly in terms of friendship and relationships but you can also understand others and sympathize with them. You will listen to those who are troubled and do what you can to help them, though woe betide anybody who later lets you down because you never forget and you rarely forgive.

You tend to be suspicious of new people and you need them to prove themselves worthy of your affection before you can allow yourself to become really involved with them. In business, you prefer to meet people face to face rather than dealing with someone who you cannot see and get to grips with. You are an expert at digging out other people's secrets but your own secrets are strictly a private matter. Even when drunk or gossiping, you manage to keep your head screwed on and your skeletons locked in your cupboard.

You can be one of the most charming members of the zodiac when you need to, and when you ally this to your persistence and persuasive talents you can also become one of the most successful salespeople of the zodiac. You are also the most loyal and helpful of friends, but in personal relationships, you moodiness and tendency to be self-absorbed can bring problems. When upset, you can overreact to such an extent that you damage the relationship, and if you do this once too often, you may destroy it. Jealousy and possessiveness is another problem, because once you consider someone to be yours, you never ever really let them go again. Worse still, you can cut off your own nose to spite your face.

Trust is an important matter to you. You like to be trustworthy yourself and you need to be able to rely upon those who you choose to love or to work with. If this trust is betrayed, you can become a dangerous enemy. You may simply cut a person who has let you down out of your life. Your own standards are high, so you work hard and you are honest and you hate to be considered second rate. You may prefer to work behind the scenes as a second in command, allowing a more charismatic person to take pole position, but you are often the power behind the throne.

You have a wonderful sense of humor and your sense of the ridiculous means that you are highly amused by those who put on airs and graces. Your chief faults are possessiveness and moodiness. You can be extremely unpleasant (even cruel) when you are in the wrong mood and the reason for your unpleasantness is not always obvious to others. Worse still, you yourself may not know why you are upset! The other side of the coin is that you can be the kindest, most understanding and helpful person in the zodiac when you feel like it. However, your loved ones really should be issued with a calendar at the start of each year so that they know in advance when to duck.

You love to surprise people. This may be in the form of coming home with an unexpected gift for your partner, or even booking a lovely holiday and only telling the family about this later. On the other hand, you can sometimes overdo this and shock the whole neighborhood. One day my Scorpio mother came to visit. She walked into the kitchen where I was peeling potatoes for lunch and she dropped an enormous and very realistic toy spider onto the back of my hand. Hard luck, mom, spiders don't worry me, so the joke didn't have the effect you were hoping for!

The Scorpio Child

This is not the easiest child to bring up, but he can be one of the most rewarding. He is intelligent, intuitive and quick to react, but also sensitive and understanding, except for the occasional flashes of temper. You will need to give him his own space and time. This child will enjoy playing in a secret den in which he can hide away from the world. He may be noisy and outgoing or silent and watchful, but either way he keeps his real thoughts and feelings to himself. Somewhere along the line (perhaps in previous life), he has learned that the world is a tricky place and that too much trust or openness is dangerous.

Your child's later career choices may well involve investigation and diagnosis, so medicine or forensic work might appeal, as would a career in the police or the law. He may be attracted to the sea, and thus to a life that involves ships and sailing. Scorpios also make excellent psychiatrists, sales people or business people, while some are attracted to various forms of complementary medicine or hypnotherapy.

Sex and the Single Scorpio

Yours is an all or nothing sign, so you may want sex frequently or be happy to spend long years without it. Your feelings are passionate though, so when you combine an urge for sex with deep and abiding love, you go all out for love. You can use casual sex as an outlet for frustration but this is not really what you want - so let us leave this subject and look at relationships.

Marriage and Partnership

You take your relationships very seriously and are uninterested in casual flings - the superficial and trivial doesn't offer enough for you. The desire for a relationship is so powerful that it transcends reality. This need for deep intimacy means that you want to possess the one who you are involved with.

You are more than capable of being sulky and sarcastic if you don't get your own way. But on the good side you can be incredibly loyal and you will give everything you have to your relationship. Your loves and hates are deep and lasting. You may enter the world of love and romance later than most but you make up for lost time as soon as you can. Where sex is concerned, you prefer to be in control. On an emotional level, you offer everything that you have and you demand as much in return. You need your partner to focus on you and to make you the center of his or her life.

Should the marriage fail, you could be cruel and vindictive, refusing to admit to any responsibility for any of the problems. However, your insight and intuition means that you usually choose the right person in the first place, so failures are pretty rare. Once you have made the decision to love someone, you devote yourself to them and love them deeply. You can be a bully, so you need a partner who can stand up to you. It is also a good idea for your partner to have supportive parents and also their own income, so that they are in no danger of being entirely dependent upon you.

With a Fire Sign Partner

You have very different views as to how you think the relationship should go. When it works, it positively buzzes with excitement, but the fire sign person might not be able to offer the level of intensity and intimacy that you need. This lover won't take kindly to your habit of hurling hurtful remarks at them when you're in a bad mood.

Scorpio/Aries

A highly charged combination but you are unlikely to enjoy the Aries habit of teasing others and the Arian lack of sensitivity can make you resentful and angry. Though difficult in the long term it could be an exciting short-lived affair.

Scorpio/Leo

You both have high standards and you both care very deeply for your children. As long as you also care very deeply about each other, this is a good combination.

Scorpio/Sagittarius
Sagittarius is generally far too inconsistent for your tastes and you won't tolerate the Sagittarian habit of complaining loudly about the fact that his or her life is not as wonderful as it should be.

With an Earth Sign Partner
You both need security in a relationship, so this can be a good combination. The quality and compatibility is there and you can understand each other, so this can result in a long term and loyal relationship. The sensual earth sign partner can also offer you the sex you require.

Scorpio/Taurus
A dynamic attraction of opposites where you go out of your way to satisfy each other, so this is a good long-term combination. You are both obstinate though, so you can expect a few clashes.

Scorpio/Virgo
This is a highly dynamic combination as your two signs have much to offer one another and you will respect Virgo's intelligence and capacity for hard work. If the Virgo partner is neurotic or hypochondriac, you won't leave them but you will simply tune their conversation out and treat it as background noise that can be ignored.

Scorpio/Capricorn
This is a partnership of two ambitious people who can establish a beneficial and pleasant relationship, as long as you have the same dreams. Capricorn's tendency to take offence at the drop of a hat will lead to arguments - and you may not be sexually compatible.

With an Air Sign Partner

This can be difficult because an air sign partner needs plenty of space while you want to cling. They enjoy change and novelty whereas you're happier staying in one place. Having said this, the air sign partner can encourage you to make the most of yourself.

Scorpio/Gemini

Gemini finds it hard to get to grips with your intensity and you find Gemini superficial. There could be a mutual fascination at the outset but a lack of understanding makes this one unlikely to go far.

Scorpio/Libra

Your passion and emotion will irritate Libra, while Libra's habit of switching off after lovemaking will drive you crazy. You want to talk while Libra wants to think, so this is not a good combination.

Scorpio/Aquarius

Aquarius finds your demands absurd and you find Aquarius almost impossible to understand. However, the Aquarian is able to ignore your moods and sarcastic remarks. This can just work if you are the breadwinner and the Aquarian has interesting pastimes.

With a Water Sign Partner

There are plenty of similarities here as you are both intuitive and emotional, and you may even have a psychic bond. At best you can give each other the emotional security that you both need but you can both become depressed at the same time.

Scorpio/Cancer

A good match, as you both need loyalty and devotion and you're able to supply one another with the security you both need.

Scorpio/Scorpio

A meeting of heart, soul and body can lead to a marriage made in heaven, or this is an explosive combination where jealousy and vicious fighting will make this a battle to the death.

Scorpio/Pisces

A highly unusual and erotic combination, where the deviousness of Pisces is well matched with your ability to manipulate.

Starting a Family

Your high energy level means that you're likely to find the early days with your new addition less exhausting than others do. You want to know everything about your new baby and it's all too easy for you to not allow your child any space. Even the youngest child may want to sit and think some of the time. You can be inflexible so you may resent the changes to your routine that a young child forces on you. However, you love your child with great passion, so once you accept their point of view life becomes much easier.

As a Scorpio mother-to-be, you have an overriding desire to look into the goriest of details about childbirth from day one. All those secrets, the mystery of birth... you want to know it all. No matter how cool you may appear on the surface, you develop a passion for this child even before it is born. There will be times when you feel put out by the way that a pregnancy takes control of your life, and the effect that it has on your sex life can get you down at times. Once baby is about to arrive, you give you heart and soul to the experience and everything else is forgotten.

With a Fire Sign Child

This is not an easy match because you are both strong willed. You are both sensitive and easily upset. You must learn to curb your tongue because, if you habitually criticize your child he will rebel. A child's anger quickly subsides and is forgotten - unlike yours, which simmers and resurfaces over and again.

With an Earth Sign Child

There may be a clash of wills as the earth sign child's stubbornness can create problems, and it may be difficult for you to make your offspring to change his mind.

With an Air Sign Child

This child needs freedom and there will be times you will find this hard to understand, especially when they are old enough to want to escape from home and to go exploring by themselves.

With a Water Sign child

This is a strong combination with a deep emotional connection, and you may know what this child is feeling even before he tells you. You will find it difficult to keep secrets from this child. Water sign children are very sensitive, so if things are not going well in your relationship, they will pick this up.

Adult Relationships

This is where we look at your relationship with your parents or with parental figures in your life. Like all your relationships, those with parents and so on are intense, so they can comprise love, hate or a confusing mixture of both.

With a Fire Sign Parent

This parent can motivate you, and also give you encouragement. He or she will help you to conquer your fears and to overcome obstacles and lend an ear when you have problems to discuss. He may become irritated at your lack of haste and he may try to pressurize you into doing things his way.

With an Earth Sign Parent

This parent will offer help whenever you need it, and his stability and reliability are something that you can depend upon. He will generally go along with your plans and wishes, and he will be happy to involve himself in your family when this is needed.

With an Air Sign Parent

This parent will leave you in peace and not get involved in your life. On the face of it, this can be a good thing, but you may prefer more help when you have problems. These parents can seem a little distant and uninterested.

With a Water Sign Parent

The bond between you and this parent is strong, and this is a wonderful thing as long as your partner is happy with it, but if your parent cuts your partner out of the equation, there will be trouble. Another problem is that you and your parent may wallow in self-pity at times.

In-laws and Similar Relationships

These relationships can be tricky at the best of times but it will be down to you to make them work. If you respect and like these adults, all will be fine, but if you cannot do so, you won't hesitate to let them know.

With Fire Sign In-laws

Happily these in-laws will leave you to get on with things most of the time, but if they take it upon themselves to interfere in your life, this will cause problems for both parties. If they upset you, you will not forgive or forget, and you could end up causing a feud between your family and theirs.

With Earth Sign In-laws

With mutual respect, this can be a good relationship but they will want to involve themselves in your life to some extent and you may not be altogether happy with this, so you must gently and kindly set a few boundaries. If there is enough in common between yourself and them you could actually develop a real friendship with these relatives.

With Air Sign In-laws

They are rational, detached and somewhat distant, so this might work on a social level, but you cannot expect much more than this. If you want help or involvement, find a water-sign friend to give you this rather than expecting it from these people.

With Water Sign In-laws

This can be a strong match that works so well that you may even live together as one family at times. It is so easy to become involved in each other's lives that you may end up having no time for your own.

Grandchildren

Yours is such a hard-working sign that life can be quite hard while your own children are young, because that is when you make the most effort out in the world of work. Later on, you are in a far better position to spend time with them, and not feel as though there are other things that you should be focusing on. Thus, for you, this is a grand opportunity to catch up on the fun times, aided by the fact that you can be far more relaxed with grandchildren than you were with your own offspring.

With Siblings

Yours is such an all-or-nothing sign that your relationship with brothers and sisters is either excellent or dreadful. Whatever pattern of mutual support or jealousy and contempt is formed when you are young remains - with or without a veneer of civilization - later in life.

Choosing a Pet

Being such an all or nothing sign, you either love animals or loathe them. If you love them, you can cope with large animals, those that need to be trained to behave properly or even real oddities such as snakes and reptiles.

Your Vehicle

You may fancy riding around on a motorcycle when you are young - and even when you are not so young. Otherwise you prefer a practical vehicle that won't let you down. Small automobiles don't appeal to you and they won't be able to hold all the stuff that you love to carry around with you.

Sagittarius

23 November to 21 December
Gender: Masculine
Element: Fire
Quality: Mutable
Planet: Jupiter
Symbol: The Archer, or Centaur

Your Character

The symbol for your sign is that of an archer on horseback or the mythological half-man, half-horse centaur, but have you noticed that the arrow that is depicted is not pointing at anything in particular? This can represent an aspect of your personality because you may fire arrows haphazardly and chase off after them - with no particular destination in mind. Your fate and destiny is a little like playing roulette, you take your bet and then see what happens. You may not be able to make up your mind about what you want to do in life, so you are open to a variety of options.

You have a fierce sense of justice, which means that you can fight for the rights of others, although you find it much harder to fight for your own rights. Fresh ideas and new challenges fascinate you, so you tend to look for new avenues to explore, but it sometimes takes time before you find the right one. You dislike being tied down or being backed into a claustrophobic situation. Being a good judge of character, you can sum people up quickly and make snap decisions about matters that involve other people, but you are not so good when it comes to understanding yourself. In your dealings with others, you are honest and you usually come to the point right away.

Although astrology books don't often mention this, you can be good at art and crafts, due to your imagination and your creative flair. Those of you whose birthdays are rather late in the sign and fairly close to that of Capricorn are certainly extremely good at do-it-yourself jobs and such tasks as electrical wiring, plumbing and so forth. You learn quickly and you don't shrink from a challenge, so you can go into home improvements or even find work in this kind of practical field.

You have a strong interest in philosophy and cultures of different people and places. Mind, body and spirit subjects such as astrology or psychology appeal to you. Many of you reject the religion that you were brought up with and find something later that you can really believe in.

One drawback is that you may feel that you are destined for better things than life is showing you. Alternatively, you may have great dreams and ambitions but you may lack the commitment and motivation to carry them through. As a friend of mine says, Sagittarians can lack "follow-through". This can lead to dissatisfaction for some but others of your sign are extreme optimists for whom the cup is always half-full.

The Sagittarius Child

This child has a strong will and a definite personality of his own which will you will find difficult to mould. He is a quick learner and sometimes this causes problems, because this child can become bored with the pace of lessons at school, switch off and fall behind. Some give up and drop out of the education system altogether. The trick is to encourage him and also to find a teacher that understands the child's need to find learning exciting and interesting. He may gravitate towards subjects such as history and religion but he will also show a strong mathematical bent. This child tends to do things very quickly and not always particularly thoroughly, so he must be taught to finish what he starts and to do things properly.

It is likely that this young person will want to take a gap year from college or university to travel and to explore the world. Indeed, as far as careers are concerned your youngster may gravitate to the travel industry so that he can take advantage of the opportunities for travel that this affords. Publishing and journalism are good careers choices too, as is any form of teaching, training or sporting careers - especially if these also include coaching. Dealing with horses or horse racing may be another career route.

Sex and the Single Sagittarian

Some of you are extremely shy and slow when it comes to dating, relationships and sex. You may lack the confidence to ask someone for a date or you may simply find the implications of future commitment unnerving. If you are this kind of Sagittarian, you can only expect to get anywhere either if the other person makes the first approach or if you have one of those experiences where you meet someone and simply know that this is the one and only person for you. Some of you give up on sex and dating altogether and live out your lives in celibacy, possibly sublimating your sexual or love needs into your family, religion or a cause.

If you belong to the other variety of Sagittarian you're likely to flirt a great deal, although you may not take your flirtations very far. You can be dynamic and exciting in a love relationship as spontaneity comes naturally to you and you are easy to get along with. Your honesty means that you will tell your friends about your lover - down to the last intimate little detail. Yours is the sign of the hunter, so the thrill of the chase is important and you are happy to tell a lover what you would like to do in bed.

You may enjoy discussing the peculiarities of others, and if you are a highly sexed Sagittarius, I have it on good authority that there is nothing you won't try. You are enthusiastic when roused but overconfidence and a tendency to rush things can make you clumsy. Despite your habit of talking about everyone and everything - and freely embellishing your stories, you are concerned about what others have to say about you!

For you, sex is a fun-filled experience, involving laughter and play - and you are happy to take a trip to the countryside and throw a blanket on the ground for a change. You can be promiscuous and happy to indulge in one-night stands. You're ardent and sincere but must feel free, so commitment frightens you.

Marriage and Partnership

Sometimes a sense of adventure leads you into marriage, and if you are the amusing, freedom-loving type, the seeds are sown for a divorce almost before you've started. You're not terribly family-oriented and you will not suffer interference from relatives. Domestic activity doesn't hold much interest for you, but you prefer to be surrounded by beauty and to live in a clean environment, so you will put at least some effort into home making. While your honesty can be endearing, it can also be the downfall of a relationship. Your lover should never ask you a question if there is the slightest hint that he or she will not like the answer that you give. Remember, the stark truth can be painful.

With a Fire Sign Partner
You both move so quickly that you may forget to move in the same direction. There is plenty of excitement on offer but the fire energy that you share can be a bit hot to handle at times, and you might end up fighting one another. You have plenty in common, including boundless energy, but some compromise is essential in order to avoid this being a short-lived romance.

Sagittarius/Aries
Both of you are enthusiastic and ready to throw yourselves into a relationship with complete abandon. Your demands for freedom may cause problems if Aries begins to take the affair too seriously, but this has the potential for being a good relationship.

Sagittarius/Leo
This is a good combination for friendship but in a relationship situation Leo may be too demanding and you may not want to settle down as quickly as your Leo lover would prefer. However, there is enough in common to make this combination a possibility.

Sagittarius/Sagittarius
Common interests will help to keep you together but you might both be ready to take up any better offer that comes along, because you both suspect that the grass may be greener elsewhere.

With an Earth Sign Partner

It can be hard for your partner to keep up with you because you live life at different speeds so you will feel frustrated at times. Earth sign people can be very obstinate and while they seek to protect themselves (and you) from your worst excesses, you will see this behavior as restrictive. It is nice for you to have a partner who can take charge of the practicalities but the relationship may not be exciting enough for you.

Sagittarius/Taurus

Taurus reacts too slowly for you and he will be upset by your need for freedom. Operating at such different speeds means it's hard for you to get on well together.

Sagittarius/Virgo

Your focus is on adventure, while Virgo's is on commitment, so this makes for an unlikely match. However, you would probably remain friends after a short affair came to an end.

Sagittarius/Capricorn

You cannot offer the devotion and security that Capricorn needs, so this is an unlikely match.

With an Air Sign Partner

Air and fire makes a volatile mixture but it can work well as the air signs can offer encouragement and enthusiasm. However, air signs like to think things through before embarking on them and this could cramp your style, because you like to act on impulse. It can be lots of fun spending time together but if you want the relationship to last you will need to work at it.

Sagittarius/Gemini

This attraction of opposites offers plenty of excitement, but as neither is consistent or wants to give their all, so it may be a short-lived affair rather than a long-term relationship.

Sagittarius/Libra

This can work, if Sagittarius will provide at least a veneer of respectability. Friendship is more likely than love.

Sagittarius/Aquarius

Neither of you is necessarily looking for something long term, so you allow each other enough space to keep the relationship sparkling.

With a Water Sign Partner

This can work well in a traditional partnership where Sagittarius is the breadwinner and the water sign the homemaker, otherwise this would be fraught with problems. Water sign people need to be validated and to be told that they are doing things right and they also need permanent emotional assurance and you will find this far to wearing after a while. If you can provide the comfort and security that your water partner needs, it may work.

Sagittarius/Cancer

The Cancerian craving for security and your need for freedom don't sit together well.

Sagittarius/Scorpio

The sex will be exciting but Scorpio is possessive, so if he starts a relationship he expects it to last. You are far too inconsistent and freedom loving to cope with this. The Scorpio tendency to criticize will get you down and your tendency to be blunt will offend this partner.

Sagittarius/Pisces

You may trust Pisces far more than he or she deserves and you will end up being the one who is let down for a change.

Starting a Family

Your optimistic attitude helps you to cope with this new experience in your life. You will soon discover that company of a young baby isn't enough to keep you satisfied, so you need to keep some kind of career going while bringing up baby. However, once the child is a little older, you will play with him and to encourage him to learn new skills.

As a Sagittarian woman, as soon as you discover that you are pregnant, you're convinced that it will turn out brilliantly. This is the greatest adventure you've ever been on and you love adventures. Though being sensible doesn't come easily, it's worth reminding yourself that this really isn't the time to take up dangerous sports! When the time comes to give birth, your sense of humor will keep the hospital staff in stitches!

With a Fire Sign Child

You share many outside interests and you will both love sports. However, you will need to keep your competitiveness under control, and to allow your child to win some games, or he will soon become angry and resentful.

With an Earth Sign Child

This can be a successful combination because you encourage your child to work hard, but you mustn't be too pushy because the child may not cope with the pressure. The last thing you want him to do is to drop out of school. Encourage him to cook and to make things, as he will find this easy.

With an Air Sign Child

Trying to get this child to watch a complete program on the television is not easy, and making him stick to school subjects is even more difficult so you will need to encourage your child to pay attention to detail and to persevere. It may take a while for this child to find the right career direction.

With a Water Sign Child

You will find this child very loving and supportive but you may wish that he had a little more drive and energy. He will take an interest in the things that fascinate you and he may end up sharing your hobbies. This child will not have your sporting talent, but he will be very caring towards others and you will love that aspect of his character.

Adult Relationships

We don't have quite the same kind of relationship with our parents than we had when young, so this section of the book concentrates on how you interact as an adult with your parents or with any parent-type figure in your life.

With a Fire Sign Parent

When this works well, it is a strong combination, as you can both pull in the same direction and share similar ideals, but if you disagree there can be difficulties. In many ways, you are too alike and you can both overreact when something upsets you.

With an Earth Sign Parent

This is generally a very good combination as earth sign parents offer practical help and understanding. It may be hard for you to live up to their ideals or to be as practical and sustained as they are, but no matter how much they disapprove of the things that you do in life they will always be there for you.

With an Air Sign Parent

Your parents will support you and they will be happy with your choices in life, even if they don't always agree with them. At times you will want this parent to be more helpful and more involved in your life than he or she cares to be.

With a Water Sign Parent

This is not a good combination as their emotionalism can spoil the relationship and this parent may want more from you than you can give, but he will be there to give you support when you need it. Water sign folk have long memories so they will harp on about past hurts or ancient problems.

In-laws and Similar Relationships

This next segment concerns adult relationships with in-laws and others who are part of your life, although not blood relatives.

With Fire Sign In-laws

Although you have many similarities, this can make for an explosive combination and differences of opinion are likely to get out of hand. If you can get together for holidays, sports, games and amusements this can work, but it is doubtful that you will be happy if you see too much of them.

With Earth Sign In-laws

These in-laws want to be helpful while you want to get on with things in your own way and time. Sometimes you could use some help, so it would be counter productive to explode at them for interfering, and if you run into financial problems, it's good to know that you have someone to call on. You may envy each other's talents, but why not simply accept that your talents are not of the same kind as theirs and leave it at that?

With Air Sign In-laws

You both enjoy social interaction. However much it galls you, you may need to remind yourself that the bright ideas that they come up with really are bright ideas. You can find it hard to get to grips with each other as you're so different, but with care you can complement each other.

With Water Sign In-laws

This is a difficult combination as it will be all too easy for you to offend them and you will find their brooding exasperating. They may continue to treat your partner as a child who has yet to leave home, but there are times might actually be useful - for example when you want a babysitter for a much needed night out!

Grandchildren

Now this is where you really come into your own, because there is a side to you that never really grows up. You love playing with your grandchildren and joining in their games and you can teach them and encourage them to overcome any problems that they have with their school subjects.

With Siblings

This is usually an excellent relationship throughout life, because even though you may live many miles apart from your brothers and sisters, you keep in contact with them and you thoroughly enjoy getting together with them when you can.

Choosing a Pet

Almost any animal suits you, and in fact you may prefer animals to human company. You have such an instinctive feel for the minds and hearts of animals that it is unlikely that you would go through life without having at least one pet. It hurts you when a pet falls ill or dies.

Your Vehicle

You don't need a prestige vehicle - although you would not turn one down if it was offered to you on a plate - but you do need plenty of space for your sports gear, do-it-yourself tools and equipment, your family and your pets. One of those multipurpose vehicles or an off-road, four-wheel drive automobile might be the answer.

Capricorn

22 December to 20 January
Gender: Feminine
Element: Earth
Quality: Cardinal
Planet: Saturn
Symbol: The Goat

Your Character

Like your symbol the goat, who wanders casually up a mountain, your ambition can take you to the top, and if it takes time for you to achieve your goals that is fine, because you have the patience to wait. In common with the other earth signs, you are practical, sensible and knowledgeable. You aren't short of self-discipline so boundaries or limitations actually give you a feeling of security. You rarely mix emotion with business.

There are two main types of Capricorn. One is quiet, shy, retiring and introverted, but this person is saved from dourness by having a dry sense of humor. The other type is extravert, sociable, always on the go and a good talker - although not always a good listener. Whichever type you belong to, you will be tactful and reasonably sensitive to the feelings of others. You will certainly be sensitive to your own feelings, possibly to the point where you can take offence over practically anything, and you may even take umbrage as a means of controlling others.

You are not the most innovative sign of the zodiac, so once you've decided how to do something, this may well be how your parents did it, which means that you are in danger of becoming rigid and inflexible. It's also unlikely that you would get excited over modern gadgets. I have one Capricorn friend who lives as though technology hadn't been invented. She has no television, CD player or cooking gadgets and she only recently replaced her ancient twin-tub washing machine with an automatic model!

You worry over the minutest details and some of you can fuss to the extent that if you break a fingernail you can't cope. You need to learn to look on the bright side of life and guard against being too pessimistic. You prefer to know what is going to happen during the course of your day and you may find it difficult to deal with unexpected events. Another Capricorn friend of mine asks her family and friends how many pieces of toast they want for breakfast the following day, so she can cut the bread the evening before! I don't know what would happen if, having asked for one slice, I changed my mind at breakfast and asked for two - I've never dared!

Material and financial success is important to you, so you usually achieve it. You are likely to be ambitious for yourself and also for anyone important in your life, such as your family, close friends and work colleagues. You fear poverty, so you worry about money, and the worse thing that could happen to you is to become dependent on others. Because of this you are likely to be a good saver and to handle money in a very practical and sensible way. Some of you are quite penny pinching but there are others among you who use money and position to benefit others. At work you are very conscientious, responsible and a good organizer, so you start out at the bottom of the ladder and then rise gently to the top, and you thrive in a corporate environment.

Yours is not a sporty sign but many of you love to dance, so this can be an outlet for you and a relief from all the effort that you put in to your life at work or in the home. Oddly enough many of you are quite psychic and some of you take an interest in alternative health and complementary therapies.

Although ambitious, you are a real family person who will take care of every member of your family. With luck, you remain close to your parents throughout life and you really appreciate and enjoy your partner. Needless to say, your children can expect all the love and care in the world from you. You may be a little old-fashioned in your approach to family life - but there is nothing wrong with that.

The Capricorn Child

Your Capricorn child may find it difficult to make individual friends while he is young, but he adapts well to organizations such as scouts, stamp collecting groups, dance groups and youth clubs, especially if he is allowed to take responsibility. He will do well at school, being especially quick at mathematics, physics and technical drawing. He may well be clever at arts and crafts, as he is likely to combine a flair for design with a structured approach.

Your youngster could be attracted to careers in architecture, landscaping, town and country planning and property consultancy. He may choose to buy and sell antiques because he will find it easy to recognize the designs and similarities of a given painter, designer or type of pottery. Another successful field is that of politics, law and police work. This sign is associated with wood and trees, so forestry, furniture making and carpentry might appeal.

However, above all, finance is the career where your young whiz kid will really come into his own. This is probably one of the most financially astute signs of the zodiac, so he could make a clever managing or financial director, accountant or business consultant. He will be capable of taking charge of companies, formulating successful strategies and guiding them through to prosperity.

This child will love you deeply and he will never abandon you - even when you are old and unable to fend for yourself. He will happily read to you and keep you company, while also taking care of his own family. In some ways, he is too responsible, so he must be encouraged to enjoy himself as much as possible.

Sex and the Single Capricorn

You find flirting, courting and messing around extremely unnerving. You don't have much confidence in your ability to attract others and you don't enjoy casual sex. It takes time for you to learn to trust a partner and you hate to rush into anything. Being an earth sign, you don't lack sexuality, but you are unnerved by the thought of having to do something strange or new.

Some of you stay with your parents until you are middle aged, but equally, you might marry while young - and if this is a success, you stay with the same partner for life. If it is not a success, you can slip back home to mother, and it may be many years before you take the plunge again. To be honest, dating, experimenting and looking around for short-term love doesn't suit you.

Marriage and Partnership

It takes time for you to find the right partner and you weigh up all kinds of considerations before plunging in. Your partner must be on a similar wavelength to yourself and it is an advantage if your partner can encourage you to play light sports, to get you away on holiday and to make you relax. You also need a strong partner who you can take pride in. You believe in family ties and you will do all you can to avoid divorce, but if it comes to the crunch, you won't be persuaded to go back and try again.

Your views of marriage are conservative and you are likely to adopt traditional roles within a marriage. Security is what you seek from marriage and you're ready to provide whatever it takes to make sure the two of you feel secure. You will make sure that the practicalities of life are well taken care of.

With a Fire Sign Partner

Your loyalty and devotion maybe able to make this relationship work, but your partner will need to allow you to do things at your own pace and not rush you into anything. You are both ambitious and likely to support each other's aims, so this can be quite a successful working relationship, but it is a doubtful one as far as love is concerned.

Capricorn/Aries

The Arian spontaneity doesn't sit well with your practicality and stability, but if you appreciate each other's qualities, this combination can surprise others by emerging as a serious relationship.

Capricorn/Leo

Your tendency to fuss over details will drive Leo up the wall. This is probably a better combination for a working partnership than a romantic one.

Capricorn/Sagittarius

Sagittarius doesn't offer enough devotion and he or she cannot provide the security you need, so this isn't an easy match.

With an Earth Sign Partner

This is obviously the best combination of all as you share similar likes and dislikes and your outlook is much the same. You are both obstinate, so when you need to solve problems, you may disagree on how to go about it, so you both need to learn to meet each other half way.

Capricorn/Taurus

You are both real family people and you love your home and garden. You share a love of cooking, dancing and socializing with close friends or family members, so this is likely to be a successful combination. You will sometimes need to encourage the other to spend money and to treat yourselves to something nice on occasion.

Capricorn/Virgo

Your views on home making, money and life in general are quite similar, and you may also share intellectual interests. This should be a fairly peaceful and harmonious relationship, as long as you both curb your tendency to criticize.

Capricorn/Capricorn

This can be a good partnership - highly efficient and practical but you may find yourselves getting so engrossed in material concerns that you forget all the other things in life - like having fun!

With an Air Sign Partner

Air signs are usually very flexible and adaptable and likely to change their minds at the drop of a hat, and this does not combine well with your dislike of change. It can take a while for you to build a mutual understanding.

Capricorn/Gemini

Gemini can be overwhelmed by your desire for commitment, especially if Gemini was hoping for a light hearted, uncomplicated affair.

Capricorn/Libra

Although both of you are conventional in your views, you may find Libra a bit too cool and unmotivated for your liking. However, you share an interest in domestic matters and you both enjoy family life, so this could work.

Capricorn/Aquarius

You two are very different on the surface, but if you take time to get to know one another you may find that you enjoy each other on an intellectual level. You will probably be the one who attends to practical matters, because your partner won't always be able to cope with them.

With a Water Sign Partner

This can be a success because you both need security and a happy home. You are both interested in your family, so as long as the relatives on both sides are pleasant and reasonable, you could have quite a busy home life. Water sign people like to run a small business of their own and you will be happy to support this kind of ambition.

Capricorn/Cancer

You can understand each other and you are happy to fulfil each other's needs, so this makes quite a good union. However, unless you have a number of shared interests and projects, the relationship will lack excitement.

Capricorn/Scorpio

This is a partnership of two ambitious people who either support each other's aims or fight. You are both quite stubborn and critical, so this is either a great success or a complete failure.

Capricorn/Pisces

If the Piscean is a homemaker and you are the breadwinner, this can just about work. You share an interest in your home and family and you both enjoy travel but your minds don't work in the same way, so you can lose patience with each other.

Starting a Family

Family tradition is highly important to you and your approach to child rearing is likely to be conventional. You have little patience for fads and fashions in this area and you tend to think that if a particular method worked for your parents, there is no reason why it should not work for you.

Being pregnant is a serious business for a Capricorn woman. You will think about this for long time beforehand, and once a pregnancy is under way, you will have everything organized in no time at all. You will not buy every device on offer - but what you do get is the best quality and likely to last for generations. You may have the niggling feeling that you're not quite up to giving birth or caring for a child, but that won't bother you for long.

You are a very caring parent and you will do everything in your power to ensure that your children have proper nutrition, a safe and happy home and as good an education as you can provide. If you have never given your emotions free rein, having a child will do you a great favor, because here at last is someone who you can trust and love to your heart's content.

With a Fire Sign Child

This can be a difficult combination as you can find this child's rebellious attitude difficult to deal with and he will resist any attempt on your part to dominate. You may expect him to concentrate more on education, but you will support him in any sporting or other interests that he takes up. If you can both take an interest in music or dancing, this can bring you together.

With an Earth Sign Child

This is a good combination as you have plenty in common. Don't expect your child to work as hard at school as you would like, or to be as quick on the uptake as you would prefer. Later in life, you may work together or share business interests, and even when your child is young, you may enjoy doing practical things together such as model making, cooking, gardening or designing clothes.

With an Air Sign Child

You will find it difficult to understand this youngster's carefree attitude to life. When he is in his early twenties, he will want to gallivant around the world while you would prefer to seem him settling into a job and a marriage. This is an easy combination when your child is young but when he reaches his teens and older you will find that he becomes less and less like you.

With a Water Sign Child

This child requires practical and emotional support and also help with his education, and you will be willing and able to provide all this for him. You must resist the temptation to let him hang around you once he is older or he will find it hard to detach from you and live independently.

Adult Relationships

Nobody takes care of their parents as well as you do, so you may never really detach yourself from them and they may even end up living with you. Unless there is something radically wrong, this will be an excellent relationship all round.

With a Fire Sign Parent

As long as your parent doesn't try to dominate you or run your life, this should be a good relationship. You may not have much in common but you can respect each other and enjoy the differences in your natures.

With an Earth Sign Parent

This is potentially a good match as you share the same basic personality and a similar need for security. You are both obstinate so arguments can ensue, but this is one of those relationships that will either be extremely successful or very awkward.

With an Air Sign Parent

You are not really on the same wavelength as this parent, so you will either appreciate the differences between you or find them incomprehensible. This parent will not want to be around as much as you would like, as he tends to have a life of his own. This means that you won't be able to rely on this parent on a regular basis for baby-sitting, and so on.

With a Water Sign Parent

You will help this parent out in practical ways, and he will encourage you to consider other aspects of life than housework or making money. As long as you share a few interests and you both enjoy family life, this can work well. This parent will want to involve himself in your life and you will be happy with this.

In-laws and Similar Relationships

This section deals with your relationships with adults who are attached to you but who are not blood relatives.

With Fire Sign In-laws

Although these in-laws won't find you exciting, they will be very pleased that their son or daughter has married you because they will appreciate the certainty and stability that you will bring. In their turn they'll bring some extra excitement into your life once in a while.

With Earth Sign In-laws

No problems here, in fact you will get on so well together that there is a good chance that you will even brought into the family business. They will certainly be very helpful to you in your career plans.

With Air Sign In-laws

This is not a bad combination because they won't want to interfere with your life. However, you may find that their attitude to you blows hot and cold and it can take a while for you to really work out where you stand with them.

With Water Sign In-laws

This will work most of the time but your view of life is not like theirs. You may appreciate or resent their wish to involve themselves in your life, depending upon whether you rub each other up the wrong way or not.

Grandchildren

If your grandchildren are noisy, sporty children, you will not really be able to relate to them. However, if they are quiet, studious and happy for you to teach them to cook, knit, make models and sit quietly while you read to them, this can be a wonderful relationship.

With Siblings

There is no doubt about it, you will always remain close to your brothers and sisters, and if any of them get into difficulties, they will always be able to call on you to help them out.

Choosing a Pet

You are fond of small animals, so you will probably have one or two around the house, especially if you have children. You are responsible and sensible enough to look after a pet very well.

Your Vehicle

You like fuel economy but also space, so you will take the time to look around before making a purchase. Oddly enough, this is one area where you could really splash out, because you see a vehicle as a status symbol.

Aquarius

21 January to 19 February
Gender: Masculine
Element: Air
Quality: Fixed
Planet: Uranus (also Saturn)
Symbol: The Water Carrier

Your Character

Aquarius is the free spirit of the zodiac, which means that you are always ahead of your time, and you are happy to venture into new projects and new concepts. We are now entering the Age of Aquarius, which should suit your particular talents. You are unconventional, full of spirit and occasionally rebellious, so you are someone that enjoys change and progress. There is a conservative side to your nature and this conservatism means that occasionally you may appear aloof to some people. However, this conservative attitude is frequently challenged, so it is just as well that when necessary, you can adapt your lifestyle to suit the circumstances around you.

You are very good at encouraging people to make the best of their talents and their lives and you do this with great generosity. This instinct derives from the egalitarian aspect of your nature that encourages you to help out with causes and charitable institutions such as the Red Cross and Amnesty International. This kind of activity gives you an opportunity to feel that you can be part of some form of positive action. Your symbol, the Water Carrier, is confusing to beginners in astrology because they frequently assume that you are a water sign, but this is not the case. You are very definitely an air sign with all that this implies in terms of logic and analysis rather than emotionalism. You could view your symbol as a vessel that is filled with great ideas, and also as an outflow of information.

The detachment of the sign means that you may be better at friendship than you are in close personal relationships, and you may also be so busy saving the whale that you simply don't see what is going on under your nose in your own family. One Aquarian teacher who I knew was so busy being passionate about the needs of her students that she failed to notice that her own children were desperately unhappy.

This sign is especially associated with astrology, and many astrologers are Aquarians. Some profess to hate astrology and insist that it is all rubbish. This is typical of the all-or-nothing nature of the Aquarian, because you either totally love something or can't stand it. Your opinions are strong and they are very fixed. This determination and obstinacy can stand you in very good stead when you put your mind to something, but it can alienate others and damage your own interests. The same goes for your honesty and your occasional tactless outbursts, because pointing out the faults of others to their faces isn't exactly endearing.

Being logical rather than intuitive, you can be naive about people and their motives, so you can find yourself being taken for a ride by unscrupulous types. You are so honest that you see no reason why others should not be telling the truth -

even when it is patently obvious that they are not. You can always see the wider picture but it is sometimes hard for you to see what is right under your nose.

Financial security seems to elude you, so it is just as well that you can cope with living on a financial knife-edge and you may be happy to spend money, even when you don't have any to spend. It would probably be a good idea to choose a partner who has more financial acumen than you do.

The Aquarius Child

The Aquarian child is very much a free spirit who should be left to explore his own ideas and talents and he will rebel against restriction. He may be determined to keep to a particular color or style for his hair and clothes, thus one needs a certain amount of flexibility to cope with an Aquarian youngster. He is a true freedom fighter and he may indeed go on to work in the law or some form of humanitarian aid. He is always full of ideas and so keen on new technology that he may well end up, as many Aquarians do, by working in something to do with computers. Now that computers are becoming old hat, some new area of technology will inevitably arrive and Aquarians will gravitate towards it. You will usually find an Aquarian at the head of the research and development department, so you might suggest that your child looks for careers in product development, electronics, design, precision engineering or computer programming.

Sex and the Single Aquarian

Friendship is as important to you as love to you so you tend to go for friendship first and romance later. You can be slow to express your feelings and in matters of love you may be clumsy and blundering. You have a burning need for praise and attention but above all you do not want your freedom to be restricted. It is easy to get on your right side, as you're highly susceptible to flattery. There are so many variations within your sign, that you may prefer an old-fashioned marriage or a loose kind of partnership that allows you to explore other options. Your honesty means that you are unlikely to go in for secret affairs, so your choice of lifestyle is open and honest.

When it comes to sex you're happy with almost any practice. You like to get on with things and have no sense of self-limitation. Sex is never the most important issue in relationships for you, but it is not one that you can do without. You like to have sex in unusual locations - as long as these are reasonably comfortable. You may like to watch others, and you certainly enjoy watching your partner's face during the act itself. Your combination of sexuality and intelligence means that you are one of the best lovers in the zodiac!

Marriage and Partnership

Everyone you meet is special in their own way, so it's difficult for you to find that really special someone, and you tend to avoid committing yourself for as long as possible. You are notorious for long engagements, and even when you have committed yourself, you hesitate before taking that irrevocable step. On the other hand you won't want to feel that you have missed out on an experience, so at some stage you want to marry if only for that reason. You're not naturally jealous - after all you like to have lots of friends so why shouldn't your partner? You are rarely unfaithful, partially because silly notions of romantic love aren't at the forefront of your mind. If you are tempted, you're likely to end the marriage quickly rather than engage in an illicit relationship. If the marriage becomes intolerable you can disappear overnight never be seen again. Though not possessive you can invoke feelings of possessiveness in your partner, due to your fascination with other people.

It is said that we are now in the Aquarian Age and - according to the songs of the 1960s and 1970s, free love is meant to rule. However, not all Aquarians are into wife swapping parties - though undoubtedly a few are. You may find it difficult to settle down with one person, and for this reason you may be inclined to leave it quite late before getting into family life. Having said this, there seem to be two kinds of pattern than operate among Aquarians. Some don't want to settle for family life, preferring to be free to follow whatever star they are interested in, while others do try to settle down while still young. In some cases, this works very well, and you and your partner remain together for life - this seems to be particularly so with female Aquarians. However, many Aquarians of both sexes marry young, break up and spend some time alone, and then find a real soul mate later.

Male Aquarians are not keen on children, and some are quite firm in their determination never to have any. Females often have more than the average two children and some can have quite large families. Yours is such an individual sign that it is hard to pigeonhole you or to suggest that all Aquarians do the same thing. Every one of you is an individual, and your needs, behavior patterns and relationships can vary. The most important factor is that you need space within a relationship, even to the point of having a room or a study to yourself in the home.

With a Fire Sign Partner

This is a volatile mixture but it can work well because your intelligence can be allied with the fire sign person's enthusiasm and ideas. If you share ideas you can work well together but sometimes the fire sign person may consider you a bit of a wet blanket at times.

Aquarius/Aries

Aries wants to leap in head first, while you are still considering the consequences of getting involved. It is an unlikely combination.

Aquarius/Leo

You are unlikely to pay Leo the amount of attention that he or she desires, although this can be a magnetic combination.

Aquarius/Sagittarius

Neither of you is necessarily looking for something long term so you allow each other enough space to keep the relationship sparkling.

With an Earth Sign Partner

This is not a particularly good combination as the earth sign person can be a little too stick in the mud for your liking, and they find your constant changes of mind hard to cope with. It can take a while before you build an understanding.

Aquarius/Taurus

You have totally different needs and attitudes so Taurus cannot understand why you don't want a close relationship while you may reject your partner's affection. You cannot understand the Taurean need for security, money in the bank and material possessions. Taurus can't understand that ideas are more important than money.

Aquarius/Virgo

A long-term relationship is unlikely, as you find it hard to comply with Virgo's demands. You will appreciate Virgo's intelligence, so an affair could turn into a friendship.

Aquarius/Capricorn

You are superficially different but there are some similarities, and if you take the time to get to know the Capricorn, your intelligence can mix well with Capricorn's scientific but practical approach.

With an Air Sign Partner

As long as you can grow together this can make a good combination but you may grow apart in time, so this works better later in life rather than when you are both young. You need to ensure that there isn't more talk than action.

Aquarius/Gemini

Neither of you wish to live in one another's pockets, and you will grant each other enough space for comfort.

Aquarius/Libra

You both know how to make each other feel wanted and you have similar drives, although neither of you is likely to give your whole heart to the relationship. Both of you can be argumentative so this is either heaven or hell.

Aquarius/Aquarius

More likely to be a friendship than a romance, but the friendship could lead to more later.

With a Water Sign Partner

You may find water too emotionally dependent and the water sign's need for constant reassurance would be rather wearing. This person can't understand how you can be so cool about emotional issues, and he takes your detachment and logic as lack of interest.

Aquarius/Cancer

Cancer's tendency to cling could drive you away. Cancer wishes to give, but you can be too selfish for his liking. A very stressful combination.

Aquarius/Scorpio

You find Scorpio's demands absurd and Scorpio can find you almost impossible to understand.

Aquarius/Pisces

If Pisces lets you down then they will be rejected immediately - and Pisces is highly likely to do just that.

Starting a Family

The concept of starting a family is a new skill for you to learn - and you don't see any reason why you have to do things the same way as they've been done in the past. You're ready to try any new method of child rearing and you are fascinated by the latest theories. Concentrating on providing your child with everything that he needs can led you to forget that it is your love that your child needs more than anything. Sometimes you can be a little too detached and cool about the whole thing. It's worth taking time out to simply enjoy holding your latest arrival.

As an Aquarian woman, you won't allow pregnancy to hold you back. The idea of devoting your life exclusively to another human being can be a little frightening. However, you are rational enough to realize that this is only temporary, so you happily put up with the minor inconvenience of pregnancy and the early days of childcare. The growth of technology and new ideas concerning pregnancy and birth fascinate you, and you want to take advantage of everything that is going. The time you spend in hospital gives you the chance to meet a whole new range of people, and you probably make numerous friends during this time.

With a Fire Sign Child

You will consider your child to be quite forceful and perhaps even something of a handful at times, although your laid-back nature will help you to cope with this. He will not be as ready to try a variety of experiences or take an interest in a variety of subjects as you would like, so you need to plant ideas into his head and to try to encourage him to take a wider view.

With an Earth Sign Child

You may be disconcerted by the fact that this child can be very strong willed and that he may not be interested in taking on challenges or adventures. You will also find the child somewhat clinging and keen to hang around, possibly even at an age when you consider that your offspring should have left home.

With an Air Sign Child

As far as education is concerned, there couldn't be a better match because you can enjoy studying together and looking into a myriad of interesting topics, also visiting museums and places of interest. However, your child can lose interest in a subject once the initial enthusiasm has worn off, but before becoming infuriated, think back to your own childhood and you will understand.

With a Water Sign Child

This child needs a lot of love and understanding and you may find this draining when you are tired and desperate for some time and space for yourself, although you will have to summon up the energy to give him extra attention when he needs it. When your child is grown, he will want to settle down too soon for your liking. He or she will feel ready to take on family responsibilities and to settle into boring domesticity at an age when you would prefer to see him in further education or taking advantage of life-enhancing experiences.

Adult Relationships

You are not childish. In fact, you are quite mature even when you are young and your ideas and opinions are both personal to yourself and very strong. This means that you either have a terrific relationship with your parents or an extremely difficult one depending upon whether they are on your wavelength or not. Your detachment usually means that you maintain a friendly but uninvolved relationship. You believe in live and let live.

With a Fire Sign Parent

Your lackadaisical attitude can sometimes irritate these parents, because they feel that you don't put in the energy effort that is needed for success. However, you usually manage to finish what you start, so he will be happy to support you in your interests.

With an Earth Sign Parent

This is not the easiest of combinations because earth parents would prefer you to choose a controlled and static lifestyle, and they feel that maybe you are too much of a free spirit. They may be too quick to offer their opinions but they will always be on hand with practical solutions to your problems.

With an Air Sign Parent

This is a strong relationship because you share the same element. As adults, you will become great friends but neither of you will be able to rely on each other in any practical way. This can be a good relationship for shared business interests as you have the same imaginative flair.

With a Water Sign Parent

This is not an easy blend because they want to monopolize you and they may also put emotional pressure on you. You won't find it easy to admit to this, but you will want to get out from under, to escape and go your own way as soon as reasonably possible. Sometimes it is difficult for you to find the right way to express your feelings without upsetting them.

In-laws and Similar Relationships

Your detachment and friendliness will make these relationships more successful than they are for many other signs of the zodiac. You can put up with a good deal of bad behavior by other adults, as long as they give you space to do your own thing. If an in-law insists on interfering in your life, dominating you or clinging, you will find ways of wriggling out of the relationship and keeping them at a distance.

With Fire Sign In-laws

Like you, these people are sociable, so this will work well on a superficial level. However, if they try to tell you how to live you will reject them. They admire your enthusiasm and capacity for hard work but they sometimes wish you would slow down and reflect upon things.

With Earth Sign In-laws

You don't really get on as you find these adults a little boring, and they think you are eccentric. However, if you work together to achieve something this combination can produce results.

With Air Sign In-laws

This is a successful combination because you are able to share some interests and you may even enjoy taking adventurous holidays together. There will certainly be many hours spent chatting and sharing ideas.

With Water Sign In-laws

This can be a difficult relationship, as these people will not want to let you out of their sight. It isn't that they don't trust you, it is simply that they want to be totally involved in your family. This can make you feel crowded at times so it's important to make sure that they know that you and your partner have your own lives to lead.

Grandchildren

The distance of this relationship combined with the fun of playing with grandchildren can make this a very rewarding one for all concerned. You are not particularly fond of babies, so your children may not be able to call on your services at first. However, once your grandchildren reach school age, you will thoroughly enjoy taking them out and teaching them new things.

With Siblings

You are not a bad sister or brother at all, as long as your siblings leave you alone and respect your need for a life of your own. You support your siblings in times of trouble but you may not be particularly interested in them during the normal course of events.

Choosing a Pet

Being the oddball of the zodiac, you are likely to keep snakes, reptiles, goats, rats, a horse, a donkey, an aged cow and several strange birds, so you must ensure that you can find the right kind of food and living conditions for your animals. Alternatively, being the all or nothing person that you are - you may not want to have anything to do with animals at all.

Your Vehicle

You are likely to choose an automatic transmission vehicle because it makes life easier. The more gadgets on your vehicle the better, because these represent progress. Your vehicle is a tool, so you want the features that will make it easy to drive. You may prefer one of those multipurpose vehicles that can carry a number of people in comfort and all the baggage that you don't seem to be able to manage without.

Pisces

20 February to 20 March
Gender: Feminine
Element: Water
Quality: Mutable
Planet: Neptune (also Jupiter)
Symbol: The Fishes

Your Character

People born under this sign are deep thinkers who are intuitive and sensitive. Everything that you do comes from deep roots of feeling and emotion. You are a born romantic who tends to see life through rose-colored spectacles, and you are an optimist. The sign for Pisces is two fish swimming in different directions - often depicted as being tied together by their tails on a piece of cord. This symbolizes your two sides, one of which wants to escape from your current existence, while the other wants to have it back once you have done so. Your feet are on the ground while your head is among the clouds and the stars. One part of you looks for security, while the other part follows a romantic dream. This conflicting need for security versus romance and adventure often confuses you as well as the people around you. You don't wish to refuse anyone and you fear rejection and criticism, so you often take on too much of other people's work. It is easier for you to agree to something and then try and sort things out later.

Many of you are artistic and you love to escape into a dreamy world of artistry, and even the most practical and business minded of you rely on intuition and inner instinct, but you can be impractical over details and financial matters. When times are bad you look on the bright side, although like all water signs when you get depressed you can get very downhearted indeed. You respond to the atmosphere around you, so if those around you are upset or depressed you can be brought down. Sometimes the situation is so obtuse that you don't even realize why you are upset. You are even sensitive to changes in atmospheric pressure and weather, and you don't cope too well when the weather suddenly changes. Others suggest that you should apply common sense to such things, but often this kind of remark makes no sense to you at all - common or otherwise.

You may not be artistic but you certainly need an outlet for your imaginative creativity. Many of you are self-employed, although you can work for someone else as long as they are sympathetic to your talents and your aims. You may have a creative hobby that turns itself into a career - but if you work alone, you need someone with a good grasp of admin and bookkeeping to back you up. You understand others so well that they find it hard to keep secrets from you and any apparent nosiness on your part stems from a need to understand people. Even those of you who are in practical jobs take the trouble to understand the needs of those to whom you supply goods or services. Although not materialistic in the usual sense, there are things that you hang on to for sentimental reasons, such as photos, books and your record collection.

You are naturally spiritual and you may be so religious that you take this up as a career. You will find astrologers well represented in this sign, because this is a career in which you can use your intuition and innate psychic ability. Many of you become painters and musicians and you may pursue these careers while happily allowing your partner to be the breadwinner. Although gentle, you are good in a crisis, which is partly responsible for your attraction to the caring professions or medicine. Your intuition and desire to please can also make you a successful salesperson.

You need the security of a home, and many of you choose one that is near water in the form of the sea, a lake or a river. Even if this is not so, the sea or important trips that involve crossing water is likely to be a part of your life. Some parts of your home, such as your books or the tools of your trade, will be meticulously organized while things that you consider unimportant may be left in a mess. In this as in so much else, you are unpredictable and unfathomable. I remember visiting the home of a scruffy, punkish Piscean acquaintance only to find it meticulously clean and tidy. His icebox contained very little food, but naturally, there were plenty of cans of beer - all neatly lined up!

Others consider you to be wishy-washy because you will not make snap decisions. Being a Piscean myself, people tell me that I give contradictory answers to a question - often answering yes and no or even yes/no. If I am asked to give a price for something, I may give a vague amount rather than a definite one. You find concrete choices and decisions difficult, so you rely on intuition or psychic abilities.

You don't really have a temper and you prefer to scuttle away rather than face up to a confrontation. It is hard for others to fight with you because you don't react - rather you absorb things and get hurt and upset. You can be touchy though, so if someone catches you off guard, you can snap back at them - although this is quickly over. You often leave things unsaid or only give half an answer - not because you have anything to hide but you hold back those things that you know others don't want to hear.

The Pisces Child

The Pisces child is extremely sensitive and he needs a lot of reassurance. He is imaginative and he may play with imaginary friends. He is interested in music and literature and he will use books and music as a way of avoiding contact with people. He will even shy away from himself. This child is born to care for others so he will be drawn to work in a caring profession, medicine or counseling. His intuition is so strong that he may be drawn to astrology and psychic subjects.

This child prefers to deal with friends one at a time, and he avoids organized groups. It often takes him a while to find his true vocation. He has little belief in himself and he badly needs validation, approval and encouragement. This child has great affinity for animals, and may gravitate towards a career that involves them. He has an especial affinity with cats. He needs to be gently drawn back to reality while at school because he can spend too much time gazing out of the window or retreating into daydreams.

This child may be old before he is young. His physical development in terms of height and size will not be fast but there is something wise and ancient about his mentality. The chances are that he will go through a very difficult childhood in which he has to cope with difficulties in a way that other children don't, and he may take on responsibility for himself and for others at an early age. For those who believe in reincarnation, Piscean children tend to show the attributes of having lived through many lives. This child's experiences of a painful or disjointed childhood this tends to affect the way he approaches life. There is always some kind of karmic pattern from the past to be endured. The inner isolation and differences in experience that child has from those who surround him helps to develop his imagination and his unique individuality. Even as a child he understands more than adults around him realize.

Sex and the Single Piscean

Being a born romantic, you can fall totally and hopelessly in love at the first kiss. Sometimes you become infatuated and fall in love with the idea of being in love more than with the actual person, and this kind of response leads you into affairs before you know what has happened. Everyone knows when you are in an affair because you are no good at keeping secrets. Being imaginative, emotional and sympathetic you have a strong desire for excitement and you find it hard to resist temptation, but you really should be in a settled relationship because you need grounding.

You tend not to initiate sex and you rely upon your loved one to tell you what he or she wants, and your response automatically adjusts to your partner's. Your sexual staying power is in direct relation to the amount of encouragement you are given - and you may enjoy sex in water! You're not deliberately unfaithful, but you can find it hard to say no - and you love to make others happy. You judgment in matters of love can be poor. Your willingness to listen and sympathize means that you may not notice that the other person is falling in love with you, so you can find yourself sliding into a relationship simply because you haven't the heart to refuse. When this happens, you are even capable of wearing a mask and acting like a happy lover when in reality you are not.

Marriage and Partnership

Whether you marry early or late is dependent on who you meet. You are romantic rather than practical and you may leave such sordid things as making and organizing finances to your partner. Your haphazard nature means that you may not keep the home or family running smoothly, so your partner will need to love you as the soul mate that you truly are. You don't have a jealous nature but you do expect loyalty. A possessive partner won't understand the way that you run around after others. It is just that if you receive a cry for help, you answer the call - even if this means temporarily neglecting your duties in the home. You may be so willing to help others that they can invade your life, take up your time and treat you like a mug. You may be the last to leave the office on Christmas Eve when everyone else has gone home.

You have a love-hate relationship with your own company. You are rarely alone because you have many friends and you also marry when young. You hate to feel boxed in, so you need space and solitude, but you need to know that your partner is nearby. Being romantic and an idealist, you may find it hard to stay faithful. You tend to keep your eyes on the horizon in case there is someone better for you out there. You want things to stay as they are at the start of a relationship - full of enthusiasm and desire, and you may find it difficult when romance gives way to routine matters such as finances and family life.

With a Fire Sign Partner

You have very different views as to how you think the relationship should go. When this works, it positively buzzes with excitement, but your partner might not be able to offer the level of intensity and intimacy that you need.

Pisces/Aries

Your subtlety is completely alien to the Arian's direct approach, so this is an unlikely combination.

Pisces/Leo

It is difficult to combine Leo's morals and values with your lack of practicality and loyalty, but you appreciate the support that Leo can offer you.

Pisces/Sagittarius

You both love to travel and explore and you also share spiritual interests, so this can make for quite a good relationship, especially if the Sagittarian has a practical streak.

With an Earth Sign Partner

You both need security in a relationship so this can be a good combination. You are compatible and you can understand each other, so this could result in a long term and loyal relationship.

Pisces/Taurus

An initial attraction is likely and you share an interest in music, singing or artistry. If you can cope with the fact that Taurus likes life to be well organized and you don't, it can work.

Pisces/Virgo

Although Virgo is an earth sign, this person tends to live in the world of logic and intellect, while you rely upon your feelings. Virgo also enjoys rescuing those who are emotionally needy - and you need to be rescued, so this can work out.

Pisces/Capricorn

Capricorn is far too shrewd to be taken in by Pisces, so this can introduce reality into the situation. Your natures are polar opposites, but sometimes opposites attract.

With an Air Sign Partner

This can be a difficult combination, as the air partner needs plenty of space, while you want to cling. Logical Gemini and Aquarius will find you puzzling but Libra can live in a fantasy world and he shares your artistic streak, so there may be enough in common to make this one work - just.

Pisces/Gemini

Whereas Gemini lives in the head while you dwell in the world of feeling. It would be difficult for you to find enough common ground on which to meet. Also, Gemini can be demanding and a misery which will depress you.

Pisces/Libra

You are both creative and you are both also very attached to your homes. However, neither of you are particularly faithful and both of you can be unrealistic, so this relationship is unlikely to stand the test of time.

Pisces/Aquarius

If you let Aquarius down you will be rejected immediately - and you are highly likely to do just that.

With a Water Sign Partner

You share the same emotional traits and you can encourage each other. You may also share a strong psychic bond but you both get depressed at the same time so you need to be careful that you don't drag each other into a deep sea of despair.

Pisces/Cancer

There is a deep emotional contact and the two of you may feel comfortable together, but you tend to float off and get involved in people or projects outside the home, which can make your Cancerian partner feel unsettled.

Pisces/Scorpio

A highly unusual and erotic combination, where your deviousness is well matched with the manipulative tendencies of Scorpio.

Pisces/Pisces

Your combined vagueness makes for a chaotic lifestyle, but you are both sociable and you love your children, so you might make something of this. On the other hand, you can drift into alcoholism together.

Starting a Family

You may not actually sit down and decided you want to become a parent at a specific moment in time. It is more likely that this happens and you simply go along with the idea, and being flexible you have little difficulty in changing your lifestyle to accommodate the new arrival. If anything, you can focus on your newborn so much that you forget to allow space for yourself.

As a Pisces woman, the sacrifices you need to make during pregnancy don't worry you at all because you fell in love with your baby the minute you learned you were pregnant. You may have a few doubts about how you're going to cope and you are likely to have a few weepy moments, but on balance you'll sail through pregnancy and you will be full of dreams about how perfect life will be once the little one arrives. You would like the whole birth experience to be just as much a dream and the idea of giving birth in water is likely to appeal to you more than to anyone else.

With a Fire Sign Child

There may be clashes as your modes of thinking are often quite different. Also, you are keen to do the best for your child, but he could run you ragged with his demands.

With an Earth Sign Child

This can work well, as you are able to give the child the emotional security that he needs, but you may find his will power, and desire to ignore your wishes trying at times. You may find your child unwilling to try new things and you will need to encourage him to do so, and while it is not in your nature to push a child, you will need to make the effort.

With an Air Sign child

This child needs his own space while you want to help, so his independent nature may feel like rejection to you. He will not always wish to take your advice because he needs to make his own mistakes and to learn and discover new things for himself.

With a Water Sign Child

There is a strong psychic link between you, and you will often share the same sensitivities, instincts and talents. This child enjoys being cared for and he may try to remain under the umbrella of your protection too long. You will need to fight against your own naturally caring instincts in order to ensure that he finds his own way in the world without being overprotected.

Adult Relationships

You may get on well with your parents and continue to see plenty of them, but if you are on different wavelengths, you can lose touch with each other.

With Fire Sign Parents

Fire sign parents can motivate you but they can also become angry and frustrated at your lack of haste. They aim to encourage you, but they end up pressurizing you into living their way.

With Earth Sign Parents

This can work because earth signs offer stability and assistance. They want to carry out your wishes and to be involved in part of your family and this can be a great help on a practical level.

With Air Sign Parents

This can be difficult from your point of view, as your parents will tend to leave you alone and not wish to get involved. Although good in one way, they can be a little distant and cold.

With Water Sign Parents

Although the bond is strong, you may need to detach yourself from these parents because your partner can feel left out of the relationship. Your parents will offer you support but you may also have to support them in their turn.

In-laws and Similar Relationships

These people will fit into your life if they are sympathetic towards you, but if there is the slightest chance that they wish to dominate or criticize you, you will find a good reason to move your family to the other side of the world.

With Fire Sign In-laws

These people think you're far too vague and may try to make you into something that you are not. If they are happy to let you get on with your life in your own way, that is fine but if they criticize or interfere too much, you may even break up a marriage in order to get away from them.

With Earth Sign In-laws

These people will want to take charge of your home and family and they consider that you should be more organized than you are. You will resent this, and depending upon circumstances you will either ignore their comments or drift away from the marriage.

With Air Sign In-laws

Although you share many ideals this can be a difficult relationship. You see them as part of your family, whereas they have their own lives to lead and they can find your enthusiasm for joining in a bit restrictive. You need to let them know that you're there when they want you but you must guard against boring them.

With Water Sign In-laws

You can get on very well with these in-laws and you may even enjoy family holidays and outings with them. In some cases, you live in each other's pockets or you rely upon each other more than is healthy.

Grandchildren

There is no question about it - you simply adore your grandchildren. So much so that they could well spend more time at your house than at their own homes. It is an amazing fact that many Pisces people end up taking their grandchildren into their homes.

With Siblings

If your brothers and sisters are on the same wavelength as you, and if they are happy to have your company, this stays a strong relationship. Otherwise, you drift away from them.

Choosing a Pet

You don't need to go out and look for a pet, because you can be sure that sooner or later, one will come looking for you. If there is a real lame duck around, you will take it in.

Your Vehicle

Many Pisceans never learn to drive, while some only do so later in life, when it becomes an absolute necessity. Having said this, some of you drive from an early age - and then have accidents because you drive too quickly.

Your vehicle must be large enough to carry your children, grandchildren, animals, travel kit, a wardrobe, the kitchen sink - and a week's supply of food and drink!

Conclusion

I hope this book has given you food for thought, and that it has helped you to understand the people in your family and those around you a little more. In this book, we have only been able to concentrate on the sun sign, because that is something that everyone knows. In the deeper forms of astrology, we look at all the other planets, in addition to the sign that was rising over the horizon at your time of birth (the rising sign), and much more.

Astrology has taught me to allow my own family the space they need to develop their own personalities, ideas and life-styles. On occasion, I have had to control my own Piscean tendency to overprotect my loved ones - and especially to give my Gemini wife space and freedom in which to dream up and implement her own ideas. I have also needed to control my own need for constant reassurance.

I am often asked which is the best sun sign for someone to choose as a lover. There is no "best" sign for anybody, as a relationship depends on all the planets and factors in two people's birthcharts, and I have never come across a pair of charts that are a perfect fit. Relationships are about the fascinating business of exploring other people, along with all that is easy or difficult for us to live with. Astrology is not about choosing a partner or planning a family based on a specific sun sign, but for learning about the energies of the signs and the relationships between them, and then working with them and perhaps rectifying their weaknesses.

When one takes things a step further than sun sign astrology, the positions of Venus and Mars have a special influence on relationships, as they indicate our approach to romantic love (Venus) and passion (Mars). The calculations involved in finding the positions of these planets and what they signify, go beyond the scope of this book, but I hope that this book encourages you to take your astrology a step further, so that you can investigate these and other planets, and their significance on your own birthchart.

Adam Fronteras
Website: www.adamfronteras.co.uk
Email: adam@adamfronteras.co.uk
Also: www.sashafenton.com

Index